Oliver Mackwoo~~d~~ ~~and C~~
association with **Par**~~k Thea~~
Birmingham Rep~~ertory Thea~~

What
Shadows

by Chris Hannan

What Shadows opened at Park Theatre, London, on
27 September 2017

The play received its world premiere in The STUDIO at
Birmingham Repertory Theatre on 27 October 2016

What Shadows

by Chris Hannan

Cast

SAEED/BOBBY/SGT SHERGAR	Waleed Akhtar
SULTAN/DOCTOR SHARMA	Ameet Chana
ROSE CRUICKSHANK/	Amelia Donkor
JOYCE CRUICKSHANK	
CLEM JONES	Nicholas Le Prevost
ENOCH POWELL	Ian McDiarmid
SOFIA/PAMELA	Joanne Pearce
GRACE/MARJORIE JONES	Paula Wilcox
YOUNG ROSE CRUICKSHANK	Niyala Clarke
	Sienna Clarke
	Ami Marks
	Tsemaye Masile

Creative Team

Director	Roxana Silbert
Designer	Ti Green
Lighting Designer	Chahine Yavroyan
Original Sound Design	Giles Thomas
Video Designer	Louis Price
Movement Director	Anna Morrissey
Voice and Dialect Coach	Stephen Kemble
Casting Director	Gaby Dawes
Associate Director	Luke Kernaghan
Assistant Sound Designer	Chris Drohan
Production Manager	Chris Hay
Wigs and Wardrobe Supervisor	Cecily King
Company Stage Manager	Jo Alexander
Deputy Stage Manager	Clare Loxley

Creative Team

Chris Hannan | Writer

Recent theatre credits include: *Crime and Punishment* (co-production with Citizens Theatre/Liverpool Everyman & Playhouse) and *The Iliad* (Royal Lyceum Theatre Edinburgh); *Elizabeth Gordon Quinn* (Traverse Theatre, 1985); *The Evil Doers* (Time Out Award 1990 and Charrington London Fringe Best New Play Award); *Shining Souls*, which opened at the Traverse Theatre in 1996 and was revived by the Old Vic in 1997, winning a Scotland on Sunday Critics Award and a Lloyds Bank Playwright of the Year nomination. In 2006 *Elizabeth Gordon Quinn* was revived by the National Theatre of Scotland in its inaugural season. *The God of Soho* was staged by Shakespeare's Globe (2009) and *The Three Musketeers and the Princess of Spain* (Traverse Theatre/English Touring Theatre/Belgrade Theatre, Coventry) was nominated in the 2011 CATS (Critics' Awards for Theatre in Scotland) in four categories, winning Best New Play and Best Ensemble; he also made new versions of Ibsen's *The Pretenders* (Royal Shakespeare Company, 1991); *Gogol's Gamblers* (Tricycle Theatre, 1992) and *Stars in the Morning Sky* (Belgrade Theatre, Coventry, 2012). His 2008 novel *Missy* was awarded the McKitterick Prize for a debut novel.

Roxana Silbert | Director

Birmingham Repertory Theatre credits include: *The Government Inspector* (in association with Ramps on the Moon); *Anita and Me* (co-production with Theatre Royal Stratford East); *The King's Speech* (co-production Chichester Festival Theatre/UK tour); *Of Mice and Men*, *Khandan* (Family) (co-production with Royal Court); *Dunsinane* (National Theatre of Scotland/Royal Shakespeare Company); *A Life of Galileo* (co-production with Royal Shakespeare Company/Theatre Royal, Bath) and *Tartuffe*.

Roxana Silbert is Artistic Director of Birmingham Repertory Theatre and was previously an Associate Director of the Royal Shakespeare Company. Roxana was Artistic Director of Paines Plough (2005–2009), Literary Director at the Traverse Theatre (2001–2004) and Associate Director at the Royal Court (1998–2000).

Ti Green | Designer

Recent theatre credits include: *Time and the Conways* (CATS nomination for Best Design; co-production with Dundee Rep and Royal Lyceum Theatre Edinburgh); *The Emperor* (Young Vic/HOME, Manchester); *Miss Atomic Bomb* (West End); *The Government Inspector, A Christmas Carol* (Birmingham Repertory Theatre); *The Etienne Sisters* (Theatre Royal Stratford East); *I Am Not Myself These Days, The Spalding Suite* (Fuel Theatre); *The Funfair, Romeo and Juliet* (HOME, Manchester; Theatre Award for Best Design); *Playing for Time* (Sheffield Crucible); *Bright Phoenix* (Liverpool Everyman); *A Woman In Mind* (Dundee Rep/Birmingham Repertory Theatre); *Orlando* (Manchester Royal Exchange); *Henry VI Parts I, II* and *III* (Shakespeare's Globe); *A Midsummer Night's Dream* (Theatre Royal Northampton); *Unleashed* (Barbican); *The Resistible Rise of Arturo Ui* (Liverpool Playhouse); *Richard III, Little Eagles, Coriolanus* and *Julius Caesar* (Royal Shakespeare Company); *Revenger's Tragedy, The Five Wives of Maurice Pinder, The UN Inspector* (National Theatre); *Coram Boy* (National Theatre/Imperial Theatre, New York; Tony nominations for Best Costume and Set Design).

Chahine Yavroyan | Lighting Designer

Recent theatre credits include: *Amédée, What Shadows, Cold Calling, The Arctic Project, The Government Inspector, Anita and Me, Khandan, Tartuffe* and *Have Box Will Travel* (Birmingham Repertory Theatre); *Anything That Gives Off Light, Let the Right One In, Caledonia, Realism* and *The Wonderful World of Dissocia* (National Theatre of Scotland); *Monster Raving Loony* (The Drum); *King Lear, Major Barbara, Hedda Gabler, The House* (The Abbey, Dublin); *Dancing at Lughnasa* and *Punk Rock* (The Lyric, Belfast); *Someone Who'll Watch Over Me, Jane Eyre* (Perth Theatre); *Uncle Vanya* (The Minerva); *Bright Phoenix* (Liverpool Everyman); *A Soldier in Every Son, Measure for Measure, Marat/Sade, Dunsinane, God in Ruins, Little Eagles* (Royal Shakespeare Company); *Dr Faustus, Punishment without Revenge, Fuente Ovejuna* (Teatros del Canal, Madrid); *The Lady from the Sea, Three Sisters, A Comedy of Errors* (Manchester Royal Exchange); *Unreachable, Hope, The Pass, Narrative, Get Santa, Relocated* and *Wig Out!* (Royal Court); *The Vortex* (The Gate, Dublin); *Fall, Damascus, When the Bulbul Stopped Singing* (Traverse Theatre); *Mahabharata* (Sadler's Wells); *Dallas Sweetman, House of Agnes* (Paines Plough).

Giles Thomas | Sound Designer

Recent composer and sound design credits include: *Wish List, Yen* (Manchester Royal Exchange/Royal Court); *Contractions* (Sheffield Theatres); *Correspondence* (Old Red Lion); *I See You, Wolf from the Door, Primetime, Mint, Pigeons, Death Tax, The President has Come to See You* (Royal Court); *Pomona* (National Theatre/Manchester Royal Exchange/Orange Tree Theatre; Offie nomination for Best Sound Designer 2015); *Sparks* (Old Red Lion); *The Titanic Orchestra, This Will End Badly, Allie* (Edinburgh Festival Fringe); *Little Malcolm and his Struggle Against the Eunuch, Orson's Shadow, Superior Donuts* (Southwark Playhouse); *Outside Mullingar* (Theatre Royal, Bath); *Back Down* (Birmingham Repertory Theatre); *Lie With Me* (Talawa); *The Sound of Yellow* (Young Vic). Sound design credits include: *They Drink It in the Congo* (Almeida Theatre); *The Sugar-Coated Bullets of the Bourgeoisie* (Arcola Theatre/HighTide Festival); *The Snow Queen* (Southampton Nuffield/Northampton Royal & Derngate); *Betrayal* (I Fagiolini/UK tour); *A Harlem Dream* (Young Vic); *Khandan* (Birmingham Repertory Theatre/Royal Court); *Three Men in a Boat* (Original Theatre Company/UK tour); *King John* (Union Theatre); *Shoot/Get Treasure/Repeat* (Royal Court/Gate Theatre/Out of Joint/Paines Plough/National Theatre); *House of Agnes* (Paines Plough).

Louis Price | Video Designer

Recent theatre credits include: *5 Soldiers* (RKDC, Sadler's Wells); *MK Ultra* (RKDC/UK tour); *The Emperor* (Young Vic); *The Rotters' Club* (Birmingham Repertory Theatre); *Mavra/Renard/Les Noces* (Royal Festival Hall); *The Etienne Sisters* (Theatre Royal Stratford East); *The Funfair* (HOME, Manchester); *L'Enfant Et Les Sortileges* (Royal Festival Hall/Philarmonia); *Bright Phoenix* (Liverpool Everyman); *Orango* (Royal Festival Hall/Helsinki Festival/Baltic Sea Festival Stockholm); *Unleashed* (Barbican Theatre); *Sluts of Possession* (Edinburgh Festival Fringe/Film Fabriek Belgium); *There is Hope* (UK tour); *Amphytrion* (Schauspielhaus Graz); *Wings of Desire* (Circa/International Dance Festival Birmingham); *The Resistible Rise Of Arturo Ui* (Liverpool Playhouse); *Beside the Sea* (WOW Festival/Purcell Room, Southbank Centre).

Other credits include: Louis directed the documentary film *Beyond Biba: A Portrait of Barbara Hulanicki* (SkyArts/Sundance Channel) and is developing *Exegesis: A Very British Cult* (BBC Wonderland/November Films) and *Black Country* (November Films/Arts Council). Editing credits include: *Best* (Sundance Film Festival) and *In Mid Wickedness* (Tbilisi Film Festival). Director of Photography credits include: *5 Soldiers Installation* (Herbert Gallery, Coventry/Stadtmuseum, Dresden).

Anna Morrissey | Movement Director

Recent theatre credits include: *Richard III* (Almeida Theatre); *Soul* (Royal & Derngate Theatres/Hackney Empire); *The Absence of War* (Headlong/Sheffield Theatres/Rose Theatre); *Rise, Ages* (Old Vic New Voices); *The Quiet Room* (Echo Presents/ Birmingham Repertory Theatre/Park Theatre); *Back Down, A Christmas Carol* (Birmingham Repertory Theatre); *Circles* (Birmingham Repertory Theatre/Tricycle Theatre); *The Crucible, My Generation* (West Yorkshire Playhouse); *King Charles III* (West End/Almeida Theatre/New York); *World of Extreme Happiness* (National Theatre); *Pericles, Antony and Cleopatra, The Grain Store, The Drunks, The Tragedy of Thomas Hobbes, I'll Be The Devil, Cordelia Dream, Marat/Sade* (Royal Shakespeare Company); *Dunsinane, Caledonia* (National Theatre of Scotland); *Bus Stop* (New Vic Theatre); *My Dad's a Birdman* (Young Vic); *Boeing Boeing, The Village Bike* (Sheffield Theatre).

Opera credits include: *Macbeth* (Welsh National Opera); *Swanhunter* (Opera North/The Wrong Crowd); *Salome, Hansel and Gretel* (Northern Ireland Opera); *The Magic Flute* (NI Opera/Nevill Holt); *Macbeth, The Flying Dutchman, Noye's Fludde* (NI Opera/Beijing Music Festival/MISA Shanghai); *Elisir D'amore, The Barber of Seville, Manon Lescaut* (Opera Holland Park). Director credits include: Associate Director for *We Are Here* (National Theatre); *Elizabethan Christmas* (Hampton Court); *Beating Heart Cadaver* (Finborough Theatre).

Stephen Kemble | Voice and Dialect Coach

Recent theatre credits include: *Love for Love, Queen Anne, Titus Andronicus, A Mad World, My Masters, Candide, Wolf Hall/Bring Up the Bodies, The White Devil, The Seven Acts of Mercy* and *Snow in Midsummer* (Royal Shakespeare Company); *What Shadows, Tartuffe, A Life of Galileo, Of Mice and Men* and *The Government Inspector* (Birmingham Repertory Theatre). Over the last eleven years he has been a voice coach for the Royal Shakespeare Company, including work for their London and Lincoln Center Festival, New York, seasons. In addition to the classical repertoire, he has coached many productions of new writing, including *Little Eagles* by Rona Munro, *A Life of Galileo* by Mark Ravenhill, *Dunsinane* by David Greig, all directed by Roxana Silbert. Stephen has just completed work on the West End transfer of *Queen Anne* now running at the Theatre Royal, Haymarket.

In 2006 Stephen graduated with distinction from the MA Voice Studies programme at the Royal Central School of Speech and Drama, and in 2011 he became a Designated Linklater voice teacher. Text and voice coaching has subsequently become a significant part of his working life.

Luke Kernaghan | Associate Director

Recent theatre credits include: *Unplugged* (National Theatre of Scotland); *Edward II, The Man Of Mode* (Arts University Bournemouth); *Códice Ténoch* (Compañia Nacional de Teatro de Mexico/Royal Shakespeare Company); *Redcrosse* (Royal Shakespeare Company); *Heartbreak Beautiful* (Theatre Royal Plymouth); *The Urban Girl's Guide to Camping, No Way Out (Huis Clos)* (Southwark Playhouse); *Vantastic/Lobster* (Ovalhouse); *Rebels and Retail* (Trafalgar Studios); *The B File, The Rover* (Etcetera Theatre). Associate or Assistant Director credits include: *The James Plays, Dunsinane* (National Theatre of Scotland); *The Homecoming* (Jamie Lloyd Company); *Richard III, A Soldier in Every Son* (Royal Shakespeare Company); *Novecento* (Donmar Warehouse).

Luke is an Associate Director of the multi-award winning Australian company Big hART, collaborating on *Namatjira* (Southbank Centre, London); *Hipbone Sticking Out* (Canberra Centenary Theatre/Melbourne Festival); *Blue Angel* (Tasmanian International Arts Festival) and *To a Different Drum* (WHS). Luke gained an MA in Directing from the Central School of Speech and Drama, and trained on the National Theatre of Great Britain Director's Course.

Gabrielle Dawes | Casting Director

Gabrielle Dawes is a freelance Casting Director; and Creative and Casting Associate for Jonathan Church Productions.

Recent casting includes: TV development casting for Hat Trick Productions on *Whatever Happened to Zimraan?* by Alistair Beaton; *What Shadows* for Birmingham Rep at the Lyceum Theatre, Edinburgh & Park Theatre, London; Season Casting Associate for the 2017 Theatre Royal Bath Summer Season and Casting Director on *Racing Demon, North By North West* and *Lady in the Van.*

As an Associate of Chichester Festival Theatre from 2006–2016, Gabrielle cast over 45 productions including *Taken at Midnight, Singin' in the Rain, Private Lives, Neville's Island, The Resistible Rise of Arturo Ui, The Browning Version/South Downs, Yes, Prime Minister, Taking Sides, Collaboration* (all of which transferred to the West End), *King Lear* (and BAM New York), *Macbeth* (and West End, BAM and Broadway), *Stevie* (and Hampstead Theatre), *Top Girls* (and Trafalgar Studios) and *Bingo* (and Young Vic).

Further West End theatre includes: *Dead Funny* with Katherine Parkinson, Ralf Little, Steve Pemberton and Rufus Jones, *Hobson's Choice* with Martin Shaw, *The Importance of Being Earnest* with David Suchet, *Blithe Spirit* with Angela Lansbury, *Cat on a Hot Tin Roof* with James Earl Jones and Adrian Lester, *The King's Speech* with Charles Edwards, *Three Days of Rain* with James McAvoy, Nigel Harman and Lyndsey Marshal, *A Round Heeled Woman* with Sharon Gless. Other theatre includes: *What's in an Name* (Birmingham Rep/Mark Goucher Ltd); *The Norman Conquests* (Old Vic and Broadway); *All About My Mother* (Old Vic); *Top Girls* (Out of Joint tour); productions for Hampstead Theatre, Headlong, and Sheffield; *Caroline, or Change, Elmina's Kitchen, The Pillowman* and *Coram Boy* (National Theatre 2000-2006).

Future casting includes: *What's in a Name?* West End transfer; 2018 Theatre Royal Bath Summer Season.

Television credits include *Macbeth* directed by Rupert Goold, Harold Pinter's *Celebration, Elmina's Kitchen* by Kwame Kwei-Armah. Films include *Perdie* (BAFTA award for Best Short Film) and *The Suicide Club.*

Chris Drohan | Assistant Sound Designer

Recent designs include: *9 to 5* (Gatehouse); *Tenderly: The Rosemary Clooney Musical* (Wimbledon Studio); *Ready Or Not, The Lamellar Project* (both and UK tour), *New Nigerians, La bohème* (Arcola Theatre); *The Mirror Never Lies* (Cockpit Theatre); *After Three Sisters* (Jack Studio Theatre); *Tonight at the Museum: Charlie Chaplin* (Cinema Museum); *'Tis Pity* (Tristan Bates Theatre); *The Pursuit of Appiness* (RADA Festival); *Phoebe, Shock Treatment* (King's Head Theatre); *The Marvellous Adventures of Mary Seacole* (Edinburgh Festival); *In the Gut* (Blue Elephant Theatre); *All Or Nothing* (VAULT Festival and UK tour); *Dr Angelus, Don't Smoke in Bed* and *The One Day of the Year* (Finborough Theatre); *Spring Awakening* and *Seussical* (Chelsea Theatre); *Resolution* (The Space/Etcetera Theatre); *The Drunken City* (Tabard Theatre); *Roaring Trade* and *Finders Keepers* (Park Theatre); *Stiching* (White Bear); *Counting Stars* (Old Red Lion/Assembly Edinburgh); *The Social Notwork* (Lion and Unicorn/Camden Fringe). As a Composer, Chris has recently written a new score for *The Beggars Opera* with Bobby Locke at the Jack Studio Theatre, and composed for a BBC Radio Drama Production of *Andromache.*

Cast

Waleed Akthar | SAEED/BOBBY/SGT SHERGAR

Recent theatre credits include: *What Shadows, Cold Calling: The Arctic Project, Back Down* (Birmingham Repertory Theatre); *Fracked!* (Chichester Festival Theatre/UK tour); *Wipers* (Leicester Curve); *Velocity* (Finborough Theatre); *The Kite Runner* (Nottingham Playhouse); *Re:Home* (The Yard); *A Midsummer Night's Dream* (Tooting Arts Club); *Under 11's* (Soho Theatre); *Love Match* (Cheltenham Everyman); *Make and Model: Radar Festival* (Bush Theatre); *Betrayed* (Tron Theatre); *Black I* (Kali Theatre); *Gladiator Games* (ETC, Germany); *Screwface* (Tristan Bates Theatre).

TV and film credits include: *Bucket, Dustbin Baby, Tyrant, Three Girls, Casualty, Edge of Heaven, Doctors, Law & Order UK, Miss You Already, Salmon Fishing in the Yemen, Night Bus, 90 Minutes, Sparks and Embers, Sidney, Lipstikka, The Chop, Diary of a Jihadi, Scratch, Tonight.*

Waleed is a resident member of the Actors for Human Rights network.

Ameet Chana | SULTAN/DOCTOR SHARMA

Recent theatre credits include: *Anita & Me* (Birmingham Repertory Theatre/Theatre Royal Stratford East); *Happy Birthday Sunita* (Watford Palace Theatre/UK and international tour); *The Djinns of Eidgah* (Royal Court Theatre); *Back of the Throat* (Old Red Lion); *Behind the Image: The Spiral* (The English Stage Company); *Bollywood: Yet Another Story* (Riverside Studios); *Helmut* (Traverse Theatre/Soho Theatre); *Papa was a bus conductor innit* (Lyric Hammersmith); *Balti Kings* (Tamasha Theatre Company); *Ready or Not, Dusky Warrior* (Stratford East); *Skeleton* (Soho Theatre); *The Dice Game* (Nottingham Playhouse); *Voices in the Wind, Wicked Yaar* (National Theatre).

TV and film credits include: *My Jihad, Doctors, Casualty, The Empress's New Clothes, EastEnders, Holby City, Goodbye, Mr Steadman, The League of Gentleman, Roger Roger, The Accused, The Bill, Teenage Health Freak, Trendy, The Black Prince, Unhallowed Ground, Jab Tak Hai Jaan, Run, Fat Boy, Run, It Could Be You, Ramji Londonwaley, Another Day, Bend It Like Beckham, Wild West.*

Amelia Donkor | ROSE CRUICKSHANK/JOYCE CRUICKSHANK

Recent theatre credits include: *Villette* (West Yorkshire Playhouse); *Vassa Zheleznova* (The Faction/Southwark Playhouse); *The Fruit Trilogy* (WOW Southbank Centre/ West Yorkshire Playhouse); *Richard III, My Last Duchess* (The Faction/New Diorama Theatre); *Robin Hood, Wanted!, Mother Courage, Manchester Lines* (Manchester Library Theatre/Lowry); *I Have A Dream* (Polka Theatre); *Home Death* (Finborough Theatre); *Six Seeds* (Told By an Idiot/National Theatre of Great Britain).

TV credits include: *Guilt, EastEnders, Casualty, Doctors, Wizards vs Aliens, Holby City, Emmerdale, Trial and Retribution, The Bill, The Trial, Hollyoaks.*

Nicholas Le Prevost | CLEM JONES

Recent theatre credits include: *Winter Solstice* (Actors Touring Company/Orange Tree Theatre, Richmond); *How The Other Half Loves* (West End); *The Rivals* (Arcola Theatre); *Man and Superman* (National Theatre of Great Britain); *Love for Love* (Royal Shakespeare Company).

TV and film credits include: *Father Brown, The Jewel in the Crown, Brideshead Revisited, Camomile Lawn, Inspector Morse, Foyle's War, Agatha Christie's Poirot, Shakespeare in Love, Clockwise, The Girl in a Swing.*

Nicholas is the founder of The Wrestling School, a theatre company that explores the relationship between language, performer, and audience through the work of Howard Barker. Radio credits include *HR* (BBC Radio 4, Nigel Williams); *Maigret* (BBC Radio 4, George Simenon).

Ian McDiarmid | ENOCH POWELL

Recent theatre credits include: *What Shadows* (Birmingham Repertory Theatre); *A Life of Galileo, The Merchant of Venice, Henry V, Macbeth, Measure for Measure, The Tempest, Much Ado About Nothing, The Danton Affair, Destiny, Dingo, Days of the Commune, Schweik in the Second World War, The War Plays, The Party, Downchild, The Castle, Crimes in Hot Countries, That Good Between Us* (Royal Shakespeare Company); *Faust, Parts I & II* (Watermill Theatre); *Timon of Athens* (Chicago Shakespeare Theatre); *Emperor and Galilean, Tales from Hollywood* (National Theatre); *The Faith Machine* (Royal Court); *The Prince of Homburg, John Gabriel Borkman, Pirandello's Henry IV* (Donmar Warehouse); *Be Near Me* (National Theatre of Scotland/Donmar Warehouse); *Six Characters in Search of an Author* (West End/Chichester Festival Theatre/Sydney and Perth Festivals); *Faith Healer* (Booth Theatre, New York; Tony Award winner); *The Embalmer* and *Faith Healer* (Critics' Circle Award); *The Tempest, The Jew of Malta, The Doctor's Dilemma, Ivanov, Tartuffe, The Government Inspector, The Cenci, School for Wives, Volpone* and *Creditors* (Almeida Theatre); *Insignificance* (Olivier Award); *Seduced, The Love of a Good Man, Hated Nightfall* (Royal Court Theatre); *The Black Prince* (West End); *Don Carlos, Edward II, The Country Wife* (Manchester Royal Exchange).

TV and film credits include: *Britannia, Utopia, 37 Days, Margaret, City of Vice, Spooks, Elizabeth I, Charles II, Crime and Punishment, All the King's Men, Cold Lazarus, Karaoke, Pity in History, An Unsuitable Job for a Woman, Great Expectations, Touching Evil, Rebecca, Hillsborough, Heart of Darkness, Chernobyl: The Final Warning, Selected Exits, The Young Indiana Jones Chronicles, Inspector Morse, The Nation's Health, The Professionals, Last Night Another Dissident, Macbeth, Creditors; Star Wars, Episodes I, II, III, V and VI, The Lost City of Z, Sleepy Hollow, Restoration, Dirty Rotten Scoundrels, Gorky Park, The Awakening, Dragonslayer, Sir Henry at Rawlinson End, Richard's Things.*

From 1990–2002 Ian McDiarmid was joint Artistic Director (with Jonathan Kent) of the Almeida Theatre, London, transforming it into an international producing theatre of world renown (Evening Standard Award for Outstanding Achievement in Theatre).

Joanne Pearce | SOFIA/PAMELA

Recent theatre credits include: *A Room with a View* (Theatre Royal Bath/UK tour); *Kean* (Apollo Theatre); *How Love is Spelt, A Place at the Table, Shang-a-lang, Unsuitable for Adults, Love Field* (Bush Theatre); *A Woman of No Importance, Life After George, Arcadia, The Entertainer* (West End); *Ancient Lights* (Hampstead Theatre); *Therese Raquin* (Chichester Festival Theatre); *Pain of Youth* (Gate Theatre: Time Out Best Actress); *Serious Money* (West End/New York); *The Lion, the Witch and the Wardrobe, Little Eyolf, Cymbeline* (Helen Hayes Award), *Hamlet, Henry IV, The Alchemist, The Theban Plays, The Dybbuk, Twelfth Night, The Plantagents, The Plain Dealer, The Master Builder* (Royal Shakespeare Company: Evening Standard nomination).

TV and film credits include: *Messiah, Murphy's Law, The Jury, Silent Witness, Lovejoy, For the Greater Good, Way Upstream, The Two Gentlemen of Verona, The Comedy of Errors, Jumping the Queue, Morons from Outer Space, Whoops Apocalypse, Murder East, Murder West.*

Director/writer credits include a new translation and dramatisation of Virgil's *Aeneid, Lord of the Flies, Idylls of the King, Alice in Wonderland, Wind in the Willows, Children of the Night* (Oxford Playhouse).

Paula Wilcox | GRACE/MARJORIE JONES

Recent theatre credits include: *What Shadows* (Birmingham Repertory Theatre); *Kindertransport* (UK tour); *Great Expectations* (Vaudeville Theatre/UK tour); *Bea* (Soho Theatre); *Canary* (Liverpool Everyman/Hampstead Theatre); *Dreams of Violence* (Soho Theatre/Out of Joint); *La Cage Aux Folles* (Playhouse Theatre); *The Queen and I* (Vaudeville Theatre); *General Review of the Sex Situation* (Jermyn Street Theatre/Lewes Live! Literary Festival); *Anyone Can Whistle* (Bridewell Theatre); *The (Female) Odd Couple* (Apollo Theatre); *The Memory of Water* (UK tour); *The Comedy of Errors* (Regent's Park Open Air Theatre).

TV credits include: *Living the Dream, Upstart Crow, Mount Pleasant, Moving On, Boomers, Still Open All Hours, Jonathan Creek, Doctors, Rock & Chips, A Touch of Frost, Emmerdale, Green Green Grass, Down to Earth, Murder in Suburbia, The Smoking Room, Viva Las Blackpool, Holby City, Merseybeat, Footballers Wives, The Queen's Nose, Man About The House!.*

YOUNG COMPANY MEMBERS

Niayla Clarke | Niayla is excited to play the character Rose as she believes this is a great experience. She enjoys acting and singing and regularly attends weekly theatre club with Haringey Shed.

Sienna Clarke | Sienna is ecstatic about being cast for *What Shadows*. She has always dreamt of being part of a professional production. She enjoys all aspects of performing arts and also enjoys swimming and watching movies.

Tsemaye Masile | *What Shadows* marks Tsemaye's stage debut with a professional company. She loves writing, plays the guitar and piano, and hopes this experience will inspire her theatre ambitions.

Ami Louise Marks | Ami is very excited to be a part of her first professional play and can't wait to make her first appearance in the production *What Shadows*. Ami attends an all-girls school in North London and she enjoys expressing herself through drama and dance.

The Year was 1968...

Leaving aside the fact that Enoch Powell never actually used the phrase 'rivers of blood', his incendiary speech to a Conservative Association meeting in Birmingham on 20 April 1968 did not come out of nowhere.

Powell was addressing the concerns of, he claimed, 'hundreds upon hundreds' of people who had written to him about the impending Race Relations Act, which would be signed into law on 25 October.

Powell in fact spoke of being 'filled with foreboding; like the Roman, I seem to see "the River Tiber foaming with much blood".' His reference was to the Latin poet Virgil's epic *Aeneid*, but the press latched onto it immediately and it was quickly dubbed the 'rivers of blood' speech. Ironically, Powell was sacked from his shadow cabinet job soon afterwards, but by then the debate was firmly in the public domain and polarised opinion sharply.

The Race Relations Act was the Labour Government's response to an increasing influx of Commonwealth immigrants, many of whom suffered discrimination and violence at the hands of a minority who were satirically caricatured by the likes of Alf Garnett. The then home secretary, Jim Callaghan, told MPs they had 'rarely faced an issue of greater social significance for our country and our children'. In March, the Commonwealth Immigrants Act had been rushed through to restrict the number of Kenyan Asians arriving in Britain after a sudden surge, and the Race Relations Act was intended to counterbalance the earlier legislation by protecting newly arrived migrants.

But unrest and division in 1968 were hardly restricted to the island nation of Great Britain. Across Europe, revolutionary movements sprang up in opposition to a variety of perceived threats; in response, governments of all political shades introduced measures ranging from riot police to outright military suppression.

It was a far cry from the previous year's 'summer of love', when hippies wore flowers in their hair, campaigners marched to legalise pot and The Beatles released *Sgt Pepper's Lonely Hearts Club Band* at the height of their powers. By contrast, 1968 was, perhaps, the year of disillusionment: students rioting in Paris and elsewhere, political unrest across the globe and the escalation of war in Vietnam.

It was a far cry from the previous year's 'summer of love', when hippies wore flowers in their hair

One of the earliest manifestations of political activism came in Czechoslovakia in January. After being appointed first secretary of the Communist Party, reformist Alexander Dubcek acted swiftly to wrest back as much power as possible from the Soviet Union, which had essentially run the country since the end of the Second World War. He introduced a host of reforms that were designed to restore liberal democracy, but it was an effort that was doomed to disaster. By August, the Soviet machine had grown tired of non-violent Czech resistance to its control and sent in the tanks. Half a million troops occupied the streets as Czechoslovakia was brought to heel. It would be another 20 years before Václav Havel's Velvet Revolution ended Communist rule once and for all. Meanwhile, in France, around 800,000 people took to the streets of the capital on 13 May in protest against the government of Charles de Gaulle. Begun by students ten days earlier, the movement turned into a one-day general strike, with protesters complaining about police brutality during the preceding riots. Over the next two weeks, the country was paralysed as the direct action spread, culminating in the prime minister Georges Pompidou ordering tanks on to the streets. Perversely, a month later, voters overwhelmingly backed de Gaulle in the election that had been forced by the protests.

In America, where San Francisco had been the focus of flower power, opposition to US involvement in the Vietnam War reached its peak in 1968. Marches, protests and campaigns were launched as the military stepped up its operations on the other side of the world. Although it would be another year before it was publicly revealed, the My Lai massacre became a symbol of horror of that devastating conflict. The outrage occurred on 16 March when, according to the BBC: 'In the course of three hours more than 500 Vietnamese civilians were killed in cold blood at the hands of US troops.' There was trouble on American home soil too. 4 April saw the assassination of Martin Luther King in Memphis, Tennessee. The acclaimed civil rights leader and Nobel Peace Prize winner – best known for his famous 'I have a dream' speech in 1963 – was murdered by James Earl Ray. The killing sparked riots in more than 100 US cities and prompted president Lyndon B Johnson to plead: 'I ask every citizen to reject the blind violence that has taken Dr King, who lived by non-violence.'

Dr King's was not the only high-profile assassination to rock America that year. Senator Robert Kennedy – younger brother of the murdered president John F Kennedy – was himself murdered in the early hours of 5 June at the hands of Palestinian gunman Sirhan Sirhan. The killer, who is still serving a life sentence in a Californian jail, was believed to have carried out the attack in protest at Kennedy's support for the state of Israel.

Race was thrown into the spotlight again in October, when two American athletes staged a controversial 'black power' protest at the Mexico Olympic Games. Tommie Smith and John Carlos were gold and bronze medallists in the 200-metre race and both held a gloved hand aloft during the playing of 'The Star-Spangled Banner', the American national anthem. The symbolic statement was intended to highlight continuing racial discrimination in the United States but, perhaps predictably, it prompted an immediate backlash. While many in the black community hailed the pair as heroes, they were condemned by the national team and expelled from the Olympic village.

In culture, 1968 saw the release of the so-called 'White Album' by The Beatles, although it was officially known simply as *The Beatles*. Featuring tracks such as 'Ob-La-Di, Ob-La-Da' and 'Revolution', it was marked by friction as Yoko Ono stuck close to John Lennon in the studio and the Fab Four quarrelled endlessly among themselves. But it was also the year of *Hair*, the hippy musical that transferred to the West End after a successful run on Broadway. Capitalising on the abolition of theatre censorship in

September 1968, the production included nudity and drug-taking, and won mixed reviews from the press. It didn't stop the show being a huge success.

Other notable events in a tumultuous year included the death of racing driver Jim Clark in a Formula Two race at Hockenheim; West Bromwich Albion winning the FA Cup with a Je Astle goal; the death of iconic blind role model Helen Keller at the age of 87; the release of *2001: A Space Odyssey*, *Rosemary's Baby* and *Planet of the Apes*; Manchester United becoming the first English club to win the European Cup; the launch of the first manned Apollo mission; and the election of Richard Nixon as US President.

With unrest, disquiet and tension predominant in the air, the stage was certainly set for Enoch Powell's most notorious speech...

Photography © Mihaela Bodlovic

In Conversation...

We chat to Designer TI GREEN and Video Designer LOUIS PRICE about how they collaborate to bring their ideas to the stage.

Where do you normally begin when working on a project like What Shadows?

TG: I start by looking closely at the text, which in this case suggests many locations, and is rich in visual imagery. There were many practical physical requirements, and also many layers of poetic thinking to work with. Finding a design often involves analysing and absorbing a lot of information, and then letting go of it so that there is space for the imagination to present design ideas.

LP: Video projection onstage can be used in so many ways that it's important to begin with the tone and mood of the play itself. In the case of *What Shadows*, we looked at the imagery referred to throughout the play (water, shadows, the British landscape), and also the structure that uses two separate time periods to tell the story.

How have you worked together on the set and video design for the show?

TG: Our focus has been looking at how the video imagery can support the locational needs of the scenes and, more importantly, explore and expand the reoccurring visual imagery of the text.

LP: The idea to use video to create atmosphere, time and mood came organically through the design process. Fairly early on it was decided that there would need to be another element, that could achieve a magical quality alongside the set design and the lighting, and also to tell the story.

TG: We have had several meetings over the course of the last few months, also involving the director and the writer, in which we have honed our thoughts and shared imagery. Louis will take this material forward and develop it in his own way, to create the large amount of material needed to project a continuous, evolving, visual and emotional landscape across the back of the stage.

How have your initial thoughts and ideas materialised through the rehearsal process?

LP: When the play is being rehearsed, things always shift and change. In this case, the process of creating the imagery for the show opens up new ideas, and new textures. One has to hope that it all fits together during the technical rehearsals!

During the creative process, what challenges have you faced with this production?

TG: This is a play that is set across 25 years in multiple locations, from Scottish shore to Wolverhampton interior to hospital rooftop. The theatre that we originally designed for was the studio space at Birmingham Rep, which meant that there wasn't much infrastructure available for scene changes. We had to build our own 'backstage' journeys so that the cast could get from one exit to another entrance unseen. There was no wing space beyond this, or the ability to fly from above. This 'limitation' provided the impetus to find a single design solution for the whole play, with physical changes kept to a bare minimum of adjustments to furniture, props, lighting and projection. As ever, it was the limitation that has offered the solution.

LP: A lot of the material has to be filmed specifically for the show, so this opens up quite a lot of challenges. For example, to create the watery shadow imagery, we had to film in the studio (and work in collaboration with the lighting designer) with the actual elements (light, water) to capture them correctly for the show.

Would you say you have a particular style in your design work and how has this altered when collaborating together?

TG: My style is often described as 'minimal' or 'deceptively simple', which tends to mean that a lot of work has gone into reducing a design to its essentials. Working with Louis over the last several years has opened my eyes to the enriching possibilities of incorporating video. I love the fact that he is not precious about what kind of screen I give him to project on to, so that he will happily project over the top of surfaces and structures that have independent significance, and which can come to life in their own way when not projected on to. I am always inspired by the filmic and poetic qualities of his work, which are often not literal and bring an emotional quality to the visual world of the production.

LP: My background is in documentary film-making. I prefer to create imagery for stage that feels real, and palpable, so I try to avoid overly digital imagery if I can. I love the feeling that the video work onstage can have the same sense of tactility that can be achieved through the other (and more established) elements. Working with Ti is great, as she creates designs that really intoxicate the audience with texture, atmosphere and magic, and fit in with a more analogue aesthetic.

What have you enjoyed most about working together to create the design for What Shadows?

LP: It's always fun working with Ti, as I know that my work will help tell the story, and not be marooned in a void. There is always the challenge of creating imagery that can live up to the quality of the design, but that's where the fun lies.

TG: The best bit has yet to come – having it all onstage in the technical rehearsals and having the time to make all of the elements work together.

Producers

Oliver Mackwood Ltd (OML)

OML was created to develop and manage high-quality live entertainment in the UK and internationally. The company was established in 2013 and is based out of the Noël Coward Theatre in the West End of London.

Current productions include: *What Shadows* (Park Theatre), and *Vixen*, in collaboration with English National Opera, touring internationally in London, Finland and China.

Previous productions include: *Sand in the Sandwiches* (Theatre Royal Haymarket, and on tour in the UK); *Mack and Mabel* (Chichester Festival Theatre); *The Rehearsal*, *Pitcairn*, *Frankie & Johnny* and *Pressure* (Minerva Theatre); *Madame Rubinstein*, *Dinner with Friends* (Park Theatre); *Holes* (Arcola Theatre); and *Giovanni* (Beijing Music Festival).

Work as an Associate Producer includes: *Love's Labour's Lost*, *Much Ado About Nothing* (Theatre Royal Haymarket); *Guys and Dolls*, *Way Upstream*, *Gypsy* (Chichester Festival Theatre); *Miss Saigon* (Prince Edward Theatre); *This House* (UK tour).

OML will also act as General Manager for the production.

www.olivermackwood.com

Charles Diamond

Recent productions include the revival of Ronald Harwood's *The Dresser* (Duke of York's Theatre) with Ken Stott and Reece Shearsmith, and James Graham's 5-star show *This House* (Garrick Theatre).

West End productions include Edward Albee's *Who's Afraid of Virginia Woolf?* (Apollo; Kathleen Turner 2006 Evening Standard Award, Best Actress); Tom Kempinski's *Duet for One* with Juliet Stevenson and Henry Goodman (Vaudeville Theatre); Samuel Beckett's *Endgame* with Mark Rylance (Duchess Theatre); Noël Coward's *Design for Living* (Old Vic) and *End of The Rainbow* with Tracie Bennett (4 Olivier Award nominations and on Broadway 3 Tony Award nominations). Eugene O'Neill's *Long Day's Journey into Night* (Apollo) with David Suchet (2013 Olivier Award for Best Revival); Brecht's *The Resistible Rise of Arturo Ui* (Duchess Theatre) with Henry Goodman (2014 Olivier Award nomination for Best Actor); *Duck House* (Vaudeville Theatre) with Ben Miller (2014 Olivier Award nomination for Best New Comedy). Noël Coward's *Blithe Spirit* (Gielgud Theatre) starring Angela Lansbury (2015 Olivier Award for Best Supporting Actress), Mike Bartlett's *King Charles III* (2015 Olivier Award for Best New Play and 5 Olivier Award nominations, Wyndham's Theatre; and 5 Tony Awards nominations, Music Box Theatre); *Taken At Midnight* (Theatre Royal Haymarket) with Penelope Wilton (2015 Olivier Award for Best Actress), *The Nether* (Duke of York's Theatre) and *Gypsy* with Imelda Staunton (2016 Olivier Award for Best Actress in a Musical; Savoy Theatre).

Birmingham Repertory Theatre

Birmingham Repertory Theatre Company is one of Britain's leading producing theatre companies. Its mission is to inspire a lifelong love of theatre in the diverse communities of Birmingham and beyond. As well as presenting over 60 productions on its three stages every year, the theatre tours its productions nationally and internationally, showcasing theatre made in Birmingham.

The commissioning and production of new work lies at the core of The REP's programme and over the last 15 years, the company has produced more than 130 new plays. The theatre's outreach programme engages with over 7000 young people and adults through its learning and participation programme, equating to 30,000 individual educational sessions. The REP is also committed to nurturing new talent through its youth-theatre groups and training for up-and-coming writers, directors and artists through its REP Foundry initiative. The REP's Furnace programme unites established theatre practitioners with Birmingham's communities to make high-quality, unique theatre.

Many of The REP's productions go on to have lives beyond Birmingham. Recent tours include *What Shadows*, *The Government Inspector*, *Of Mice and Men*, *Anita and Me*, *Back Down* and *The King's Speech*. The theatre's long-running production of *The Snowman* will celebrate its 20th anniversary at the Peacock Theatre, London, this year as well as touring to Manchester, Glasgow, Southampton, Brighton and Milton Keynes.

Artistic Director **Roxana Silbert**
Executive Director **Stuart Rogers**

Thanks

For help with research Chris Hannan would like to thank Mr Sadar Ali, George Antill, Rita Antill, Nicholas Jones, Pat Jones, Mr Ram Krishan, Karamat Iqbal, Mr Mohammed Iqbal, Dr Alison Mukherjee, Rev. Supriyo Mukherjee, Eleanor Nesbitt, Jonathan Rew, Mr Banwari Lal Sharma, John Wickenden, Churchill College Cambridge, Wolverhampton Archives and Local Studies, Janet Freer-Jones and Matthew of Sutton Park. The script was developed with support from Playwrights' Studio Scotland. Thanks also go to Milli Bhatia and Sarah-Katy Davies for their efforts in the Young Rose auditions. Jan Baister and Jonny South from AKA (Marketing). Nick Pearce from Target Live (PR). Harry Totham (Production Assistant), Nicky Clarke (Chaperone), our wardrobe and backstage team and everyone at Park Theatre.

About Park Theatre

Park Theatre was founded by Artistic Director, Jez Bond. The building opened in May 2013 and, with three West End transfers, two National Theatre transfers and ten national tours in its first four years, quickly garnered a reputation as a key player in the London theatrical scene. In 2015 Park Theatre received an Olivier nomination and won The Stage's Fringe Theatre of the Year.

Park Theatre is an inviting and accessible venue, delivering work of exceptional calibre in the heart of Finsbury Park. We work with writers, directors and designers of the highest quality to present compelling, exciting and beautifully told stories across our two intimate spaces.

Our programme encompasses a broad range of work from classics to revivals with a healthy dose of new writing, producing in-house as well as working in partnership with emerging and established producers. We strive to play our part within the UK's theatre ecology by offering mentoring, support and opportunities to artists and producers within a professional theatre-making environment.

Our Creative Learning strategy seeks to widen the number and range of people who participate in theatre, and provides opportunities for those with little or no prior contact with the arts.

In everything we do we aim to be warm and inclusive; a safe, welcoming and wonderful space in which to work, create and visit.

★★★★★ 'A five-star neighbourhood theatre.' *Independent*

As a registered charity [number 1137223] with no public subsidy, we rely on the kind support of our donors and volunteers. To find out how you can get involved visit **parktheatre.co.uk**

Staff List

Artistic Director | Jez Bond
Executive Director | Rachael Williams
Creative Director | Melli Marie
Development Director | Dorcas Morgan
Development Assistant | Daniel Cooper
Finance Manager | Elaine Lavelle
Finance & Administration Officer | Judy Lawson
Sales & Marketing Manager | Dawn James
Deputy Sales & Marketing Manager | Rachel McCall
Venue & Volunteer Manager | Naomi Dixon
Technical Manager | Sacha Queiroz
Deputy Technical & Buildings Manager | Neal Gray
Café Bar General Manager | Tom Bailey
Administrator | Melissa Bonnelame
Learning Care & Access Coordinator | Lorna Heap
Duty Venue Managers | Barry Card, Shaun Joynson, Lorna Heap, Amy Allen
Bar staff | Sally Antwi, Gemma Barnett, Florence Blackmore, Grace Botang, Calum Budd-Brophy, Robert Czibi, Jack De Deney, Nicola Grant, Adam Harding-Khair, Philip Honeywell, Lasse Marten, Jack Mosedale, Ryan Peek, Mitchell Snell, Temisar Wilkey, Leena Zaher
Box Office Supervisors | Sofi Berenger, Natasha Chandra, Celia Dugua, Natasha Green, Bessie Hitchin, Holly McCormish, Jack Mosedale, Christopher Teesdale and Alex Whitlock

Public Relations | Julia Hallawell and Nick Pearce for Target Live

President | Jeremy Bond

Ambassadors
David Horovitch
Celia Imrie
Sean Mathias
Tanya Moodie
Hattie Morahan
Tamzin Outhwaite
Meera Syal

Associate Artist
Mark Cameron

Trustees
Andrew Cleland-Bogle
Nick Frankfort
Robert Hingley
Mars Lord
Sir Frank McLoughlin
Nigel Pantling (Chair)
Victoria Philips
Jo Parker
Leah Schmidt (Vice Chair)

With thanks to all of our supporters, donors and volunteers.

WHAT SHADOWS

Chris Hannan

Acknowledgements

The playwright would like to thank

Mr Sardar Ali
George Antill
Rita Antill
Nicholas Jones
Pat Jones
Mr Ram Krishan
Karamat Iqbal
Mr Mohammed Iqbal
Dr Alison Mukherjee
Rev. Supriyo Mukherjee
Eleanor Nesbitt
Jonathan Rew
Mr Banwari Lal Sharma
John Wickenden

who were generous with their time and help

and the staff of Churchill College, Cambridge and Wolverhampton Archives and Local Studies

for their kindness and courtesy.

The script was developed with support from Playwrights' Studio, Scotland.

'What shadows we are and what shadows we pursue.'

*Edmund Burke, Speech at Bristol Declining the Poll,
9th September, 1780*

4

Characters

ROSE CRUICKSHANK
SOFIA NICOL
CLEM JONES
ENOCH POWELL
PAMELA POWELL
MARJORIE JONES
BOBBY HUSSAIN
SULTAN MAHMOOD
SAEED MAHMOOD
MRS GRACE HUGHES, *later* GRACE MAHMOOD
JOYCE CRUICKSHANK
DR SHARMA
SERGEANT SHERGAR

Also PATIENT *in a mental hospital*

This text went to press before the end of rehearsals and so may differ slightly from the play as performed.

ACT ONE

Scene One

The Ends of the Earth

Kintyre, December 1992.

The shore.

ROSE CRUICKSHANK *enters. She's black, thirty-five.*

SOFIA NICOL *enters in oilskins, carrying pots and creels ashore. She's white, forty-eight. This is her piece of shore.*

ROSE. How to talk to people we hate. How to speak across the anger that divides us. You and me. England. Half the country thinks the other half is mad. Nothing to bind us together but the fact we hate each other's guts.

SOFIA. How did you find me?

ROSE. Got here at dawn. There were deer on the beach.

SOFIA. They come to lick the salt.

ROSE. So far from reality.

SOFIA. We have guns. We shoot. The children.

ROSE. You shoot the children?

   SOFIA *carries on with her work.*

SOFIA. The children shoot the deer.

ROSE. I'm teaching at Oxford now. Your old college.

SOFIA. So remote.

ROSE. The pressure to publish. My next book's about identity.

SOFIA. What's it called?

ROSE. *Who Can Tell Me Who I Am?*

SOFIA. Who can tell you who you are?

ROSE. *Who Can Tell Me Who I Am?*

SOFIA. Is there an answer?

ROSE. Nobody can *tell* me.

SOFIA. Then why are you asking? Why are you here?

ROSE. I've come to make peace.

SOFIA. I have peace. I own fourteen acres and the shoreline.

ROSE. Fourteen acres of desolation. What do you do to enjoy yourselves?

SOFIA. We throw a great funeral.

ROSE. You in oilskins. People used to say you were the cleverest woman in England. I can rehabilitate you. You're intellectually unfashionable, I'm black. We could write the book together. *Who Can Tell Us Who We Are?* England is a conflict. We could articulate the opposing views.

SOFIA *needs time to take this offer in.*

SOFIA. I read your *first* book.

ROSE. Thank you yes thank you.

SOFIA. Haven't said anything nice about it yet.

Magisterial work of scholarship. Winning the Deutscher Prize, that puts *Rose Cruickshank* up there with some *very* big names.

ROSE. When I sent the first draft to my publisher it had the snappy title *An Economic History of Immigrants to England: 1066 to the Present Day.* Seven hundred and eighty-nine pages. The publisher said, *Rose, in a bookshop why would I pick this up? I'm not going to publish unless you can tell me what it's about, in four words.* And I said

SOFIA. *Whose Idea Was England?*

ROSE. Who created the Norman churches, the Norfolk fens, the East End

SOFIA. Oxford

ROSE. the things that made England England. Sailcloth, the canvas for her ships

SOFIA. the technology of the cotton manufacturers who came from medieval with their what did the locals call the Flemish workers?

ROSE. the *blue nails*. Unforgettable detail.

SOFIA. I was spat on. That's an unforgettable detail.

ROSE. I wasn't involved in that.

SOFIA. You got me sacked.

ROSE. You justified racism.

SOFIA. You led the students, made speeches. Colleagues turned their backs on me, the broadsheets tore me to pieces. The things people said and did. It was primitive, I was *cast out*. I put my girls in the car and took off. Roof piled with stuff, left Oxford like refugees, headed for the wilds of Scotland.

ROSE. Did you forget?

SOFIA. Forget?

ROSE. Forget Oxford.

SOFIA. The sea's rich. I almost drowned once. You lose yourself.

ROSE. How did you learn?

SOFIA. You go out on other people's boats. There's money in it.

ROSE. Are you on your own now?

SOFIA. My lobster ends up in France.

ROSE. A book by Rose Cruickshank and Sofia Nicol. It'll attract attention. We can begin with Enoch Powell. His racist speech about immigrants.

Do you still have sympathies for him?

SOFIA (*she is tired of saying this*). I suggested he had a portion of the truth.

ROSE. You defended the speech.

SOFIA. I said it has never been answered.

ROSE. To describe black children he used the phrase *wide-grinning picaninnies*. Should people who use racist language even be included in the conversation?

SOFIA. Is that your decision? Who to include in the conversation and who not?

ROSE. It's almost untouchable.

SOFIA. Like me?

She's the one living in the back of beyond.

ROSE. I'm here to listen.

SOFIA. Misunderstood before I open my mouth.

ROSE. You were trying to redefine racism, you said. Isn't the definition pretty clear?

SOFIA. Black rioters burn down Asian shops. Are they racist? Nigerian English boys call Jamaican English boys slaves. Are they racist? And immigrants are often racist, they have to be to hold their communities together. They say *we're not like them, we don't eat like them, we don't think like them. We're a little different, a little better.* That's what having an identity *is*, thinking you're a little different, a little better. You don't mix with people of other identities, in marriage say. And often there's an enemy that defines you. Catholics and Protestants in Northern Ireland, or look how an atheist treats believers. He turns his nose up in disgust, his blood boils in primeval fury. We're all racist. We all belong to groups which find other groups offensive. Nice lovely liberals despise white racists, look down on white racists *like they are a lower race*. White racists are irrational, they say, no point in talking to them. Nice lovely liberals cast me out.

ROSE. You said all racism is equal.

SOFIA. Yes.

ROSE. Not when the police can kick your head in for being black. Not when whites have all the power.

SOFIA. Who in this conversation has the power?

She's the one in the oilskins.

ROSE. I'm offering to share it.

SOFIA. You took half the meaning of my life.

ROSE. I'm giving you a chance to be heard.

SOFIA. I'm wondering why.

ROSE. (I dream about you. I never dream normally.)

SOFIA. I sleep as if I'm lying on the bottom of the sea. My chickens graze on the beach, eat the sandhoppers. Their yolks are orange, red nearly. I've had two lives to your one. I'm fine.

ROSE exits.

Scene Two

The Land of Lost Content

Twenty-five years before. 1st November 1967.

Birdsong from nearby light woodland. Rooks, possibly.
CLEM JONES enters, map in hand. He's fifty-two, editor of the
Wolverhampton Express and Star, *a newspaper with a larger*
circulation than the Guardian. *He has a smile that hides more*
than it reveals and a touch of vanity (I do mean a touch) about
his looks, clothes, person.

ENOCH POWELL enters, also with map. He's fifty-five, in
country gent's flat cap, tweeds, wellington boots. They are a few
hundred yards from a pub and car park, looking for the source
of the Thames. ENOCH considers the evidence on the ground,
tries to align it with the map.

ENOCH. The Queen's Hall Barnstaple, Conservative Women Cottingham, Institute of Charted Secretaries Birmingham, *in every corner of the kingdom* my message falls on deaf ears. I'm too old to be crying in the wilderness.

CLEM. Never heard you mention your age before, Enoch.

ENOCH. Ambition makes the clock tick.

CLEM. That's the Thames there, I think.

ENOCH. To what are you pointing?

CLEM. The difference between that grass and that grass.

ENOCH. Ah.

   As a journalist, would you describe my speeches as difficult or arcane?

CLEM. The ones I've read I've never finished.

ENOCH. I have made my argument as simple as I can. The cause of inflation is not trade unions or greedy bosses, it is governments and their unlimited power to create money. Try telling our glorious leader Mr Heath. The problem with Ted is his densuousness. Offer him an idea and he turns his nose up like a small boy offered broccoli.

   PAMELA POWELL, *forty-two, and* MARJORIE JONES, *fifty-two, enter in anoraks, carrying a light picnic: flasks, sandwiches. It's cold but they're English and set on the idea of some sort of picnic.*

PAMELA (*to the men*). Have you found the Thames yet?

CLEM. There.

PAMELA. Where?

CLEM. You can see the shadow of the river in the different shade of green.

PAMELA. The girls can't throw stones in a different shade of green. I promised them the source of the Thames.

CLEM. In a month or so the water will rise, where we're standing will be a river.

MARJORIE. Shelley the poet tried to row here. With Mary
Shelley before he married her, and two friends.

MARJORIE *directs this to* ENOCH *even though he's much
further away than the others.*

ENOCH. The gravitas of autumn. The rooks, full of foreboding.
Puts one at ease. The promise of spring, on the other hand,
I always find unbearably painful.

MARJORIE. Yes.

ENOCH. The *lightness* of spring lies on one's chest with the
weight of a gravestone.

MARJORIE. They set off from Windsor, the Shelleys.

PAMELA. Was there any water in those days?

MARJORIE (*to faraway* ENOCH). Mary was eighteen, the year
before she wrote *Frankenstein*. She'd already lost a baby.
She had a dream. She rubbed her dead baby beside the fire
and it came back to life. Then she woke up of course.

Poor ghost.

PAMELA. And did they or didn't they make it as far as here?

MARJORIE. Just beyond Lechlade. There were cows standing
in the river.

PAMELA. They weren't afraid of cows surely?

MARJORIE. Cows little more than ankle deep, too shallow for
a boat.

She directs the next sentence to ENOCH.

He wrote a poem in Lechlade, *A Summer Evening
Churchyard.*

ENOCH. He wrote wonderfully about death.

MARJORIE. Death will be such a relief.

ENOCH. Sweeter. Like one's mother coming and putting one
to bed.

PAMELA. I should like to live till I'm ninety and die sitting up in bed with a brandy, watching someone dishy winning Wimbledon.

MARJORIE. You must all promise to speak nicely of me when I'm gone.

CLEM. Marjorie!

PAMELA. This is glorious. What's your favourite part of England, Clem?

CLEM. Half-six. Rabbits lost in thought

PAMELA. lost in a dream yes

CLEM. like they've been down in their holes listening to the Test Match on a transistor radio all afternoon and now they're out in the half-six light picturing Gary Sobers bowl his slow left arm chinamen.

MARJORIE. What about you, Enoch?

ENOCH. Sunken lanes in Shropshire.

MARJORIE. Wonderful. Pam, what about you?

PAMELA. Wolverhampton Train Station.

MARJORIE (*polite*). Really? Gosh. Clem met the architect.

CLEM. He suffered from clinical depression, to be fair.

PAMELA. When Enoch fought Wolverhampton for the first time, he asked me, a mere secretary, to come up from London to help his campaign; it was the Friday evening before Clem interviewed him for the *Express and Star*. My train was four hours late and there he was, still waiting for me on the uncovered platform in the pouring rain.

ENOCH (*shoulders hunched miserably*). No umbrella.

PAMELA. Enoch can't stand water on his head, he screams when you wash his hair and sulks like a soaked cat, so it was quite something.

ENOCH. Pam was a monsoon in which I was drenched.

The romance of this is acknowledged by CLEM *and*
MARJORIE, *but not overenthusiastically, they being the less
happy couple of the two.*

I did not consider mundane Black Country rain worthy of
my notice.

MARJORIE. I was stuck in a dreadful downpour with Clem last
Tuesday. Horrid, coming back from that pointless talk by
that stupid man.

CLEM. In *our* young day we swam naked in a lake in Wales.

MARJORIE. That was the fashion then. We were *neo-pagans*.
Punishing walk followed by a freezing dip.

ENOCH. Naked.

MARJORIE. Yes.

ENOCH. Very Greek.

MARJORIE. Someone ask what *I* love about England. This!
Picnics; being here with you, three. I don't have great
opportunities to talk about Shelley in Wolverhampton. I hope
that isn't snobbish of me. Isolated in some cultural backwater.

CLEM. It *is* our home.

MARJORIE. Yes!

I had a young drug addict up before me in the Magistrates'
Court last week. He said he was having a bad trip, I said *Me
too, dear.*

PAMELA. You said that out loud? Marjorie, you are absolutely
quite something.

BOBBY HUSSAIN *enters.*

BOBBY. I do beg your pardon, are you Mr Powell?

ENOCH. I believe I am, yes.

BOBBY. We saw you in the car park. Richard said not to bother
you but I wanted to thank you. You voted for homosexual
relations between consenting adults.

ENOCH. As a Tory I have long believed that where a man disposes his affections and in what manner is a matter for him and not his elected Member of Parliament to decide; but for what it's worth the love of man for man was the common practice of Ancient Greece. Socrates, Michelangelo, Goethe, were all minded to think the male form was more pleasing than the female, from an aesthetic point of view.

BOBBY. Aesthetics is not a subject we discuss in Luton. We drink in The Cock and Bull. Richard tells working-class jokes. To blend in, he says. I stand there and try to look as pale as I can.

ENOCH. I thank you for taking the time to speak to us.

BOBBY. It's been a privilege.

They give each other a little farewell bow and BOBBY *exits.*

PAMELA. Apple dumpling?

CLEM. Is it runny?

PAMELA. I'd say squishy rather than runny.

CLEM. I'm very strict about apple dumplings. That is, ah yes, exactly as it should be.

PAMELA. It's always great fun being with Enoch. You never know who you'll meet.

MARJORIE. Luton. Poor souls.

ENOCH.
>Into my heart an air that kills
>From yon far country blows
>What are those blue remembered hills
>What spires, what farms are those?

MARJORIE.
>That is the land of lost content,
>I see it shining plain,
>The happy highways where I went
>And cannot come again.

Piercing.

ENOCH. I often feel England isn't a place so much as a grief.

MARJORIE. Beauty can be a punch in the stomach.

The sound of a yellowhammer.

CLEM. A yellowhammer.

'Ah!' 'Ooh yes!' They all listen attentively.

MARJORIE. I always tell the boys you can recognise the song of the yellowhammer. Sounds like 'little bit of bread and no cheese'.

PAMELA. I must say, Marjorie, doesn't sound like that to me.

The yellowhammer.

MARJORIE. 'Little bit of bread and no cheese!'

'Little bit of bread and no cheese!'

The yellowhammer gives up.

CLEM. He's given up. You can only try for so long. If no one understands a word you're saying...

MARJORIE. Oh dear, is that the rain?

CLEM. It's on its way.

PAMELA. At least the English weather is constant. A coloured man has bought the house next door to us in Merridale Road. Changes. When a 'FOR SALE' sign goes up nowadays there's wholesale panic.

Awkwardness.

MARJORIE. Egg sandwich anyone?

PAMELA. You don't mind but when they move next door! They sublet, you see. The Pakistanis are the worst; they buy biggish houses in middle-class streets so the rest of the village can come over.

CLEM. That's how they, I mean they sublet so they can afford the mortgage.

PAMELA. There's no point being sentimental about it.

CLEM. I don't think sent don't think I'm being

PAMELA. It affects the value of one's house!

CLEM. Well yes, Pam, of course, one understands the price and everything.

I take my hat off to them, buying houses, not being content to content to rent.

PAMELA. Yes, but it's not affecting you where you live.

Eating, drinking, silence.

MARJORIE. Don't worry about the black bits in the home-made honey. Bee legs, nothing sinister.

PAMELA. Lovely. Mmm.

Eating, drinking, silence.

ENOCH. The speeches I make.

PAMELA. They seem not to reach the wider public.

ENOCH. I send a copy to Tory Central Office to be distributed to the media and

PAMELA. we suspect they sit on them

ENOCH. possibly at the behest of our glorious leader

PAMELA. Ted is more jealous of someone else getting attention than a spoiled boy. As an editor, how would you suggest Enoch might increase the impact he has on

ENOCH. Clem thinks my speeches are unintelligible.

CLEM. You're a powerful orator in a small town hall, but you don't speak to the masses, thank goodness.

PAMELA. What do you mean *thank goodness*?

MARJORIE. He's being jocular.

ENOCH. He's being dry.

PAMELA. I should hope so. We'll *pop round* some time, shall we, no great rush.

CLEM *makes unenthusiastic non-committal noises*.

Where now, Enoch?

ENOCH. I thought we might go to Fairford; one of the finest wool churches extant.

PAMELA. I'll get the girls.

PAMELA *exits*.

MARJORIE. What's a wool church?

ENOCH. In 1292 the Barons estimated that half the value of England was wool. Ordinary working men in Florence who manufactured goods with English wool would have spoken the words *Cotswold* and *Shropshire* with the same knowledgeable pleasure we name the wine-producing regions of France.

MARJORIE. Like connoisseurs.

ENOCH. They might have known the exact monastery. And with the wealth from wool, we English built some of our finest churches.

MARJORIE. You go on, we'll catch you up.

ENOCH *exits*. MARJORIE *packs a basket*.

CLEM. I would be very reluctant to help him.

MARJORIE. I thought you'd be flattered.

CLEM. Ever wondered what his ambitions are?

MARJORIE. To be Prime Minister, I imagine.

CLEM. The short cut is a terrible temptation at his age. He's been making anti-immigration speeches.

MARJORIE. He's not a racialist.

CLEM. He has a horrible poetic streak. The England he loves is the countryside, the churches, the sunken lanes. I suspect he finds immigrants unpoetic.

MARJORIE. I dislike his politics more than you, dear, but I enjoy our picnics. They keep me afloat. He won't forgive you if you turn him down.

CLEM. Yes.

MARJORIE. He's your oldest friend.

CLEM. Something chameleon about him recently. I don't trust my eyes. One might say he wants to govern England but it's more insane than that. He wants to *be* England.

MARJORIE. I don't know who you're talking about. Enoch's Enoch, he doesn't *change*. He's seen our boys grow up, he's been to their weddings, he's part of the fixture and fittings, oh for heaven's sakes

This last exclamation is because it has started to pelt down.

we can talk in the car.

Before they leave with the picnic basket, CLEM *looks around at the deceptive solidity of the field.*

CLEM. This solid field. You can't trust your eyes.

Scene Three

In My Dressing Gown

Mental hospital. SOFIA *visiting,* ROSE *enters in dressing gown. Since we last saw her she's had a five-day bender, followed by an alcohol detox in a mental hospital.*

ROSE. How did you know I was here?

SOFIA. You phoned.

ROSE. Why would I phone *you*?

SOFIA. I don't know.

ROSE. I *phoned* you. When?

SOFIA. You were very, you were distressed. You were sort of slur-slurry-slurring your words. You pleaded. And I it was three in the morning I promised to come.

ROSE. It feels like bad science-fiction telly. It's so implausible I want to switch off.

SOFIA. I can see from your point of view that

ROSE. I'm trying to apologise for you

SOFIA. sorry if you feel I've intruded

ROSE. *I'm wearing a dressing gown.*

SOFIA. yes.

   A PATIENT *comes in. He watches.*

ROSE. It's not even my own. It's the hospital's.

SOFIA. Where are your clothes?

ROSE. In my car.

SOFIA. Where's the car?

ROSE. I forget the name.

SOFIA. The name of what?

ROSE. The river. Somewhere near Dumfries. I only go on the drink twice a year. I drink for a week, ten days, then stop.

SOFIA. Why?

ROSE. The insanity. The insanity's like breaking out of jail.

SOFIA (*echoing*). You *enjoy* the insanity.

ROSE. The freedom. I went off like a rocket after I saw you. Had a bottle of vodka in the car.

SOFIA. Has anyone come to visit you?

ROSE. No.

SOFIA. Does your family know you're here?

ROSE. My work is my family. The students, the lectures.

SOFIA. Does the college know?

ROSE. No.

I haven't been sectioned. They don't even know what's
wrong with me. I'm unclassifiable. They put me in with the
alkies, which is interesting. The alpha male of the Alcohol
Unit drinks biodiesel and Castrol GTX. He's giving me life
tips. He says he's my centaur, I think he means mentor.

SOFIA. Is drinking car fluid is that a thing with alcoholics?

ROSE. It's niche. So you want to work together?

SOFIA. No.

ROSE. You're here.

SOFIA. You were desperate.

ROSE. You came.

The PATIENT *exits.*

SOFIA. You'll be back in Oxford soon.

ROSE. Yes.

SOFIA. Do you feel more clever in Oxford?

ROSE. Did you?

SOFIA. The kudos. You might question your ideas but never
your place in the scheme of things. And the river. The shade
of the alder trees on a hot day.

ROSE. Enoch Powell could be your comeback.

SOFIA. So much hate out there, so much anger. I think of
identity as an unexploded bomb. Why would I approach
a bomb with you?

ROSE. I could help to analyse it.

SOFIA. Could you help defuse it?

ROSE. We could write a manual.

This surprises and interests SOFIA. *It possibly surprises*
ROSE *too.*

SOFIA. A manual?

ROSE. How to talk to the enemy.

SOFIA. You see me as an enemy?

ROSE. That's how you see me.

SOFIA. No trickier than a treacherous coast.

ROSE. Good. If Rose Cruickshank and Sofia Nicol can defuse their hatred, anyone can. Even the English.

SOFIA. And you want to dig up the explosive subject of Enoch Powell.

ROSE. When I was a girl in Wolverhampton, he lived a hundred yards away. In his big racist immigrant speech he talks about the last white woman in a street. She lived next door to us. I'm one of Enoch's wide-grinning picaninnies.

SOFIA. I see.

ROSE. Does that appeal?

SOFIA. It's got an edge.

ROSE. I've arranged an interview with him.

SOFIA. When?

ROSE. A week on Monday.

SOFIA *considers this.*

SOFIA. Would you take me to Wolverhampton?

ROSE. Why?

SOFIA. Seems the obvious place to start. The street made famous by the speech.

ROSE. Nothing to see.

SOFIA. Is your family still there?

ROSE. My mum.

SOFIA. Well, if we're writing about identity. Mothers kind of important.

She feels her throat constrict.

Aren't they? One way or another. We remember them in our bodies. So the first thing to do is meet her, see where you come from.

ROSE. Or we do the thinking first. The theoretical groundwork.

SOFIA. Suppose someone drives a car into a river. They might theorise about it. They might say *you know I think I drink because I have low self-esteem*. They might say intellectually it's kind of interesting to read the crash as paradigmatic of a conversation between discourse and the non-discursive. But they won't go to the river and look at the crash. Hear the car's side of the story. And that's a mistake because the crash might have a theory. A different perspective from you.

ROSE. Okay.

SOFIA. Okay. I'll drive you down.

ROSE. I haven't spoken to my mother for three years.

SOFIA. Okay.

ROSE. Yes. So if that's what you want, okay.

Scene Four

Globalisation

Wolverhampton, twenty-five years earlier.

Four or five assorted chairs. The guests at the party are SULTAN MAHMOOD (*forty-odd but wearing clothes that are a bit younger, more fashionable*), *his young relative* SAEED MAHMOOD (*who's just finished a shift in a foundry*), *and* MRS GRACE HUGHES.

Silence. Except for the noise of a wonderful party next door, Lord Invader pounding out calypso classic 'Rum and Coca Cola'. ROSE, *aged ten, enters with a tray.*

ROSE. Would you like a prawn cocktail, Sultan?

SULTAN. No thank you, Rose.

ROSE. Would you like a prawn cocktail, Saeed?

SAEED. No alcohol please.

ROSE. Would you like a prawn cocktail, Mrs Hughes?

GRACE. You ought to be in bed, Rose Cruickshank.

Silence. Except for the wonderful party next door.

SULTAN. Jamaicans enjoying themselves next door.

GRACE. Glad they got summat to celebrate.

SULTAN. It's New Year, isn't it.

GRACE. We remember the dead this time o' year. My husband died in the war.

Silence. Except for the wonderful party next door.

SULTAN. You like this neck of woods, Mrs Hughes?

GRACE. I'm the only white for three streets. I got six empty rooms I could rent, but I canna let to whites 'cause whites wunna live round here, and I wunna have coloureds in the house or why'd we fight a war.

I'm off a farm, you see. Nearly by Much Wenlock I was raised. Coloureds didna exist them days. Dearie me, where was the blacks when the bombs was droppin, where was the Pakis then? They waited till the coast was clear.

SAEED. *Uncleji, eh keh bakwas hih. Goree* fucking racist, *hanna.*

GRACE. You never know what they're jabbering about, do you.

SULTAN. He is *junglee* from Mirpur, Mrs Hughes. I am from educated city Jhelum, he is taking chickens to bathroom to halal their throat.

JOYCE CRUICKSHANK *enters with a hostess trolley and Chicken Kiev.*

JOYCE. And when you all finish the prawn cocktail, I made some Chicken Kiev. Chicken Kiev?

SULTAN. No thank you, Mrs Cruickshank.

JOYCE. Oh. Chicken Kiev?

SAEED. No thank you, Mrs Cruickshank.

JOYCE. Oh. Chicken Kiev, Mrs Hughes?

GRACE. No thanks, Mrs Cruickshank.

JOYCE. Oh.

> *Silence. Except for the party next door.* JOYCE *takes her seat, hurt, close to tears.*

> Old Year's Night we call this in Barbados. All day we used to bake. Oh, the food down there.

GRACE. Oh ah. The food back then.

JOYCE. Muffin, salt bread, turnover.

GRACE. Chitterling puffs and apple cobs.

JOYCE (*in tears nearly*). Coo-coo and flying fish.

GRACE (*in tears nearly*). Red cabbage pickle and fidget pie.

JOYCE. It's not home, this.

GRACE. No. We bin robbed.

JOYCE. Robbed yes.

GRACE. Gone like the years. Dearie me.

JOYCE. Yearning.

GRACE. Yearn.

JOYCE. Mum sold some sheep to send me here.

GRACE. Afore we got wed, Dad sold off some milking cows. Gave us a tidy bit deposit for a house. When the news come, I were all by myself. I put the telegram on the dresser, unopened like. It were that quiet in the house I could hear the leaves falling on my grave. Oh ah.

> *Cheers and shouts from next door. The bells. No one in our house hugs or kisses or shakes hands. They sit where they are.*

SULTAN. If we four people could speak to each other how much history we would tell. What shall I tell you about myself. In Pakistan I am very interesting person. I have job in Irrigation Department. *Sifaad poash*.

SAEED. Sultan uncle *tahleem yafta*.

SULTAN. Educated.

SAEED. Educated men get job on buses.

GRACE. I've never liked Pakis on the buses. They want to wear their turbans now. That's one law for them and one law for everyone else, uniform's a uniform, I reckon.

SULTAN. Bloody Sikhs, isn't it, Sikh will cause row in empty house. How did you meet your husband, Mrs Hughes?

GRACE. A bus in the blackout, full o' drunk soldiers shoutin and swearin tops of their voices. It were his blush I fell for.

SULTAN. I also am shy.

GRACE. For the honeymoon he took me to Birmingham for the day. Well, it rained till evenin then it bombed. When we come out of the shelter, there was fires everywhere, buildings like wedding cakes missing a tier. We stayed up all night, tremblin head to toe, talked about the business we should start after the war. A bed and breakfast, we decided. We fell asleep talkin, top o' the bed with our clothes on. That was our wedding night. We bought the house 'cause it were a right good size for a bed and breakfast, and his regiment embarked for Egypt. But he never come back from the war, you see, so I starts lettin out rooms. Then the coloureds come and all the whites moved out. Not me. I'm not moving. We could've had a tidy business here. Oh ah. We could've had a lovely bed and breakfast.

Silence. Except for the party next door. GRACE *gets up and puts on her coat, or buttons it up if she's never taken it off.*

Best be off.

SULTAN. What about sing-song, Mrs Hughes?

GRACE. Sing-song?

SULTAN. Sing-song is matter of very grave importance. I will
sing 'I Love a Lassie'.

GRACE. Hurry up then.

SULTAN.

> I love a lassie, a bonnie, bonnie lassie,
> She's as pure as the lily in the dell,
> She's as sweet as the heather,
> The bonnie bloomin heather,
> Mary, ma Scotch bluebell.

GRACE. Surry, where'd you learn all them Scotch words?

SULTAN. I intrigue you. You see I intrigue her Saeed (he has
no idea what intrigue means), only he knows chickens.

GRACE. Oh, what sort o chickens you got in Pakistan?

SAEED. *Buhray!* Fighters.

'Buhray!' is a bad transliteration of a Mirpuri word for 'big'.

GRACE. We had silver spangled ones with teddy boy hairdos.

SULTAN. Actually chickens originally come from India
originally, Mrs Hughes.

GRACE. Happy New Year.

GRACE *exits*.

SULTAN. You see, I'm not some idiot *junglee*, I'm not some
nignog. No offence, Mrs Cruickshank.

JOYCE. Lord no offence no.

SULTAN. Thank you, Mrs Cruickshank, I always say you black
people have good sense of humour.

JOYCE (*furious*). Black? In Barbados they don't count me black.
My grandmother, she had we use to call *clear skin*. My
grandmother father was white bookkeeper at a plantation. My
gran took after him, could do accountancy quick as a fox, she
had to be quick as a fox in that rum shop she own.

Go to bed, Rose Cruickshank! I told you, you can stay up so
long as I don't see you.

She scares ROSE *off, or most of the way off.*

Black? *Rose* is black. I married down, you see, Rose is what they call black in Barbados.

SULTAN. Barbados, you have two different words for black?

JOYCE. This is great back home.

She's pointing at her face.

This means something. Here nothing mean nothing. No one know the difference. Party over now, have to put up your rent next month, been hurting myself charging so little, thank you bye.

SULTAN. Happy New Year, Mrs Cruickshank.

SULTAN *and* SAEED *go.* JOYCE *and* ROSE *are left.*

JOYCE. Always someone spoil things. Go to bed.

Scene Five

The Air That I Breathe

Wolverhampton, 17th February 1968.

CLEM *is bee-keeping in his back garden; checking his bees are still alive. He's wearing his veil, as a precaution; unlikely to be any bees flying in February.*

MARJORIE. Clem? The Powells are here.

CLEM. For heaven's sake. Why do they always turn up unannounced?

MARJORIE. They don't have a phone, dear.

CLEM. After his latest public remarks, I thought they'd give us a wide berth for a bit. I prayed for clearness at meeting for worship this morning. I'd be very *sorry* to give him up.

MARJORIE. It's not as if you disagree with him *entirely*.

CLEM. I don't believe we should talk about immigration with megaphones.

MARJORIE. He's jolly useful to you. All the inside information.

CLEM. Yes, that's why conscience, you see. He flatters my professional vanity.

MARJORIE. You're a journalist, dear. You're supposed to be shallow.

CLEM. You're speaking with a megaphone.

MARJORIE. You've made a lot of compromises.

CLEM. I know you think so.

CLEM *turns away, works with the bees*.

MARJORIE. There would be consequences for others besides yourself. Poor Pam. I dare say she has friends in London but she has no one else to turn to here.

CLEM. She'll survive.

MARJORIE *starts crying*.

MARJORIE. How are your bees?

CLEM. Dead.

MARJORIE. All of them?

CLEM. They generally live or die as a swarm.

MARJORIE. Strange when they're decomposed. Like a black mould. Sad.

CLEM. Yes. Nothing to cry about.

MARJORIE. Struggle. The lack of intelligent conversation here. Feel as if I'm gasping for air sometimes.

CLEM. It might *feel* like that for a bit.

MARJORIE. They're my oxygen.

CLEM. Send him out.

She goes. CLEM *attends to his bees.* ENOCH *comes out.*
It may not be immediately apparent to us but ENOCH *is*
consumed with rage; not against CLEM, *against his*
colleagues in the Tory Party.

I read your latest.

ENOCH. I read your editorial.

CLEM. I need to keep a balance.

ENOCH. I sensed a tension.

CLEM. Wolverhampton is like Central Africa, you said.

ENOCH. I said a constituent of mine has a daughter who is the
only white child in her class and that when I mentioned this to
the Tory MP for South Worcestershire, he stared back like I
was the MP for Central Africa. How can one part of England
be so ignorant of another part, but fifty miles distant?

CLEM. I had my reporters check your facts. Fewest number of
white children in a Wolverhampton classroom is eight, West
Park Infants.

ENOCH. You say the *fewest* number when you mean to say the
smallest number.

CLEM. It's my responsibility as a journalist to report the
accurate number.

ENOCH. Eighty per cent of the West Park Infants are coloured.

CLEM. We raised no objection to black people outnumbering
us when we governed Africa.

ENOCH. I was rebuked by the Shadow Cabinet too. They
swarmed all over me. Heath, the inexcusable Mr Hogg,
even Macleod.

CLEM. I'm surprised that remarks you made in Walsall came to
their attention. We were the only newspaper that covered it.

ENOCH. Tory Central Office sent a copy of the text to Hogg,
touching as it did on immigration. Hogg said we Tories
should discuss race in a civilised manner and glared at me.

When people use the word *civilised* they invariably mean
you don't belong in their club. I'm a grammar-school
Midlands boy; to public schoolboys I have all the character
of an Italian immigrant, or a usurper.

CLEM. You do quite often usurp their roles. It's for the Shadow
Home Secretary to speak about immigration.

ENOCH. You think I should be advised.

CLEM. They are your colleagues after all.

ENOCH. They seem to me not even my fellow countrymen.
They who hope to govern England have washed their hands
of ordinary people. They have forgotten you can only
persuade a man insofar as your thoughts are his thoughts, your
ways are his ways, you must identify with him so he will
identify with you. These last half-dozen years, when I speak to
my constituents about education, they speak about
immigration; when I mention the economy, they talk about
immigration; I say hospitals, they say immigration. Have I not
the duty as their representative to articulate the resentment
they feel, the sense they have of being overlooked.

CLEM. There's a danger you confuse them with you. *Your*
grief. *Your* resentment at being overlooked.

ENOCH. You said you'd help me communicate with the media.

CLEM. Yes, but look here, Enoch, I'm not prepared, you see.

ENOCH. Not prepared to help?

CLEM. I wasn't expecting you. I'm not ready.

ENOCH *is being rebuffed. But he decides to overlook the fact.*

ENOCH. It's like a dream. I'm the boy in the masthead, the
lookout in the rigging. I see a typhoon coming. But everyone
aboard the ship is asleep in mid-ocean.

CLEM. I know what I'm doing, Enoch. I've given this some
thought. I'm sorry.

MARJORIE *comes out, followed by* PAMELA. MARJORIE
is visibly distressed.

MARJORIE. Enoch, rescue me. All morning I've been writing
a talk about melancholia for the Samuel Johnson Society,
I keep stopping to tear it up. At this rate I'll be lucky to finish
it before I kill myself. How on earth do you finish your
speeches?

ENOCH. I keep picturing the audience.

MARJORIE. That's just the trouble. A Samuel Johnson
enthusiast is a wet blanket on fire. Can you imagine a
roomful of that? If only *you* would join the Society, Enoch.

ENOCH. Well, if you think I can add to the general gloom and
despondency, I'd be delighted.

MARJORIE. No, don't laugh, Enoch. It's pointless without you.
It's misery. I honestly think I will finish it. I've had enough.
I honestly think I will throw in the towel. Don't you think
Enoch should join the Society, Clem. If *he* were a member
I should have someone to write for. It would mean
something. I would mean something.

It's a raw appeal.

ENOCH. I should be glad to join.

CLEM. You go in, Marjorie, I'll give Enoch a few pointers.
I expect he'd like a cup of tea and a Bourbon biscuit in a bit.

MARJORIE *goes inside.*

With the press, timing's the most important thing. Saturday
afternoons, not much news then so a speech is much more
likely to be covered. And the Sundays always like to run
with something fresh. Saturday afternoon you'll get
television too, if you're in time for the six o'clock news.

PAMELA. How clever. You often have Saturday lunchtime
engagements, don't you, Enoch.

ENOCH. Conservative Associations, that sort of thing.

CLEM. And you'll generally find the Monday papers pick up on
the Sundays.

ENOCH. How do I minimise the chances of being spiked?

CLEM. One mistake you make, you bury the good stuff in the body of the speech. It's not in a journalist's character to do any work: pull out a few juicy quotes, put them on a top sheet where he can find them. TV cameras won't turn up unless they know there's a story. That's about all there is to it.

PAMELA. Goodness, easy when you know how.

CLEM. Yes.

PAMELA. This is all my fault, I pushed him to ask you. No one else we could trust, you see.

ENOCH. I'm working up a speech about a war widow. Constituent, lives a stone's throw away in a street that's been taken over by immigrants.

CLEM. Like the only white child in the classroom.

ENOCH. Yes. The only white woman in a street that's gone black.

Scene Six

Fur Coats

There is a violent knocking at the door. Demanding. Eventually GRACE *goes to answer it and* SULTAN *comes in. He hasn't used violence (narrowly defined) but he has forced his way into her house.*

SULTAN. you make me bloody angry banging the door for bloody hour

GRACE. not very gentlemanly banging me door for a twothree hour

SULTAN. you making me impossible to be civilised!

GRACE. my husband would turn in his grave he saw you here

SULTAN. you should invite me in

GRACE. I should phone the police

SULTAN. phone the bloody police

GRACE goes off, comes back with a knife.

GRACE. I dunna have a phone

SULTAN. I come here to ask you out!

GRACE. cut off from civilisation here

SULTAN. I'll show you civilisation

He goes and finds something to use as a weapon; a poker, perhaps. It needs to be something serious.

GRACE. true colours now!

SULTAN (*threatening her with his weapon*). I come here to save you

GRACE. save me, save me from what?

SULTAN. save you this half-life you are living

GRACE. (half-life) save me from *him*

She points at SULTAN.

save me from the Paki. you comes in here like a bull, demolishing everything as stands in your sex sex sex

She has an hallucination. It happens too fast for her to scream. And anyway it is no more frightening than the confrontation with SULTAN has been.

Oh my

SULTAN follows its progress; not because he sees an apparition; but he sees that she sees something. So he almost sees something.

After it's gone, she sits down.

Ai ai ai.

SULTAN. What was it?

GRACE. He were taller than the house. Like the house were nowt but a marquee and he were oh rippin it oh ah tearin it up by the roots. He pulled it out of the ground and walked away with it. Left me mother-naked. Dearie me. Hallucination, I suppose.

SULTAN *surreptitiously puts down his weapon. He sees a photo of her dead husband in uniform.*

SULTAN. What regiment your husband?

GRACE. North Staffs.

SULTAN. He meet any Punjabis in North Africa?

GRACE. Not as I know of.

SULTAN. Many Punjabis fighting North Africa. El Alamein, Sudan, all that kind of thing. Later Monte Cassino, everything.

GRACE. He mentioned tanks.

SULTAN. In Burma we have tanks in the jungle. You sleep in a foxhole. When tanks are in your neck of wood, even you don't hear them you feel the vibrations.

GRACE. You didna fight in the war, you jessie.

SULTAN. Many good things you remember. After artillery pounding, your head halfway down your neck. Then you hear pop pop pop of Japanese machine-gun peaceful you know, like noise of cricket balls on bat.

You sleep whenever you can afford it.

We have Seaforth Highlanders our brigade.

I love a lassie, a bonnie heelan lassie

They teach me that.

GRACE. I canna have my salad till you go.

SULTAN. Your husband send you letters?

GRACE. He said dunna let my brother come. He said he used a flame-thrower. Then he stopped writing me. He wrote his mam, he wrote his mother that never said a good word about him her entire miserable life.

SULTAN. He cease to write you?

GRACE. Yes.

SULTAN. Why he cease to write you?

GRACE. I don't know, do I.

In a roundabout way SULTAN *tries to suggest what might have happened to her husband.*

SULTAN. Some things you remember worse than others. I give you a for instance. Sometimes you attack Japanese position twice or thrice same day, you leave dead on Japanese perimeter wire. Third day we charge, five yards from enemy perimeter wire we run into stink of comrades' decomposing corpses. Japanese are shooting at us but we cannot shoot back, we are on our knees throwing up. We cannot advance beyond smell of corpses.

GRACE. You're making it up.

SULTAN. Maybe your *husband* saw something. Flame-throwers very bad for your sleep. Sometimes a man loses his

like when a spring is losing its spring. Can happen to anyone.

GRACE. *I* wrote *him* letters. Talked about the bombing on our honeymoon. The bed and breakfast.

She puts her salad in the bin.

(He let me down.)

That's a sentence she has never said out loud before.

SULTAN. You should eat something you enjoy.

GRACE. I *used* to be dreadful, I were in trouble along o' the chaps afore I turned fifteen. We had the farm nearly by Much Wenlock, soon as I met a chap there were dramas.

SULTAN. Where is Much Wenlock?

GRACE. Shropshire.

SULTAN. Much Wenlock. You enjoy it in your mouth I enjoy it in my mouth enjoy the words you know.

GRACE. I dare say.

SULTAN. Fog outside.

GRACE. Touch.

SULTAN. You want me to touch you?

GRACE. Touching.

SULTAN. In fog you feel England all round you. It's like you are lady wife in big-guns restaurant and fog is waiter holding your *fur* coat before you are going. That is fog in England.

He goes and gets her coat. He holds it out for her like a waiter.

GRACE. Where we going?

SULTAN. Going cinema. *Planet of the Apes*.

GRACE. Who's in it?

SULTAN. Charlton Heston.

GRACE. He's good int he.

SULTAN (*holding out the coat*). Your coat.

GRACE. I can't. I'm a war widow, y'see.

SULTAN. You don't wish anyone to see you? In this forinstance I suggest we have night in.

GRACE. You can have my home-brewed if you like.

Scene Seven

India

12th April 1968, Stratford-upon-Avon. SULTAN *and* SAEED *are dressed for the theatre. Overdressed for the theatre in men's evening wear and black bow tie.*

SULTAN. I fall in love with England before I arrive. The gardens. Top-class lady wives on lawns. Stratford-on-Avon.

SAEED (*Mirpuri/English*). *MP ki milne wastay asaan fucking theatre, hai ah?*

The above is a poor transliteration of the Mirpuri for 'To meet our MP we came to fucking theatre?'

SULTAN. I am wishing to bump into Mr Powell after play like old chums.

SAEED. Long long waiting. They waiting someone die?

SULTAN. You are lucky I bring you here, these people are big officer politicians, big officer civil servants and lady wives. Pukka. In Jhelum you copy someone you may be copying some idiot. Here you can copy word for word.

SAEED. Bloody actors dragging bloody feet. They not paying them enough. Pay more, they work faster.

ENOCH *and* PAMELA *and* CLEM *emerge on to the street. The performance has been three hours and forty minutes long, so they have a slightly stunned look as they gather themselves.*

PAMELA. Well, that was

ENOCH. Yes!

ENOCH/PAMELA. I cried. / Long!

ENOCH/PAMELA. Passionate / Terribly passionate.

ENOCH. Who is it that can tell me who I am?

PAMELA. The naked on the heath scene. Poor Eric Porter. Must be hard to say those poetic speeches in your pants.

ENOCH. The pain is almost unendurable.

PAMELA. Four hours *without brandy*. Even Alan Howard
      wasn't as handsome as he usually is. Where's Marjorie, in
      the ladies'?

CLEM. Yes. Crying.

PAMELA. Poor thing.

> SULTAN *interrupts the Powell party's exit.*

SULTAN. Mr Powell, how pleasant to bump into you, Mr
      Powell. I am old comrade, Sultan Mahmood.

> ENOCH *tips his hat in respect. After his opening 'Salaam
> Alaikum', ENOCH continues the conversation in Urdu.*

ENOCH. *Salaam alaikum.* (*Urdu.*)But forgive me, where did
      we meet?

SULTAN. I am Military College Jhelum cadet.

ENOCH (*Urdu*). I have been all over Hindustan but not to
      Jhelum.

SULTAN. Before the war they are educating us, young Muslim
      boys, to be rankandfile British India Army. Then the war
      arrive. Two million Muslim Hindu Sikh soldiers. The British
      Indian Army was a great instrument.

ENOCH. I had the honour of serving as a Colonel in
      Intelligence, GHQ Delhi.

SULTAN. You see we are old comrades in arms like I'm telling
      you. So much to reminisce.

ENOCH. Which was your regiment?

SULTAN. 16th Punjabis. Our war cry before the charge. *Allah-
      o-Akbar*, God is great. Good times and terrible pickles.
      Shongpel, C Company are suffering many bad casualties.

ENOCH. RK 6930-6983-7092-6796.

SULTAN. You remember the position?

PAMELA. Wherever Enoch goes, first question he asks is *What
      is the latitude and longitude of this place?*

ENOCH. You attacked Shongpel looking for Japanese
    Divisional HQ on the strength of the intelligence
    appreciation I wrote.

SULTAN. We are two Companies of Muslims, Company of
    Dogras from Sialkot, and Company of Sikhs.

CLEM. Did the Sikhs wear their turbans?

SULTAN. Now now, don't compare Sikhs who are fighting in
    Burma and Sikhs who are punching holes in Wolverhampton
    bus*tick*ets.

In the background MARJORIE *enters*.

CLEM. It's surely plausible to compare them where for instance
    they are the selfsame man. The turban was part of his British
    Indian Army uniform, seems odd that twenty years later it's
    not good enough for Wolverhampton Transport. Marjorie
    joined the Sikhs on their demonstration through
    Wolverhampton the other week.

MARJORIE. I'm afraid so.

PAMELA. Marjorie!

MARJORIE. Five thousand Sikhs from all over England and
    seven of us Quakers. Marching in silence like a regiment of
    soldiers through a town that's fallen.

PAMELA. Marjorie, you *are* a dark horse.

SULTAN. Well now, Mr Powell, why don't you and I meet for
    cuppa-chah sometime, talk over old war memories.

ENOCH *draws himself up as though accused and rejects the
    claims of comradeship*.

ENOCH. To live contentedly and prosperously, the one thing
    needful is self-knowledge. The inscription on the temple of
    Apollo at Delphi – γνῶθι σεαυτόν: know thyself – is an
    inescapable imperative for the individual and the nation
    alike. For over a decade I have been saying the Tory Party
    must be cured of Empire, England must be cured of Empire.
    The British Empire ended when India turned her back and

went her own way. India has its independence from England; now England must have her independence from India.

SULTAN. The tragedy is I'm in love, you see. I'm in love with England.

ENOCH. During the war I fell in love with India. My ambition was to govern her. After the war, when Prime Minister Attlee announced we were giving India her independence, I walked the streets of London all night. I was like a man after a car crash in the country, who has climbed out of the ditch back on to the road and is walking through the dark looking for help. I walked for seven hours, found myself come dawn under a railway bridge in Vauxhall where a woman was sleeping rough. She asked if I was all right and I said

England without India is like Venice without the sea.

He is close to tears or in tears. A deeply emotional man talking in public about a love affair he has never recovered from.

PAMELA. Come on, Enoch. We won't get home till after one.

PAMELA *and* MARJORIE *go.*

SULTAN, *having been rejected, gives* ENOCH *some Winston Churchill.*

SULTAN (*bitter irony*). Let us therefore brace ourselves to our duties and so bear ourselves that if the British Empire and its Commonwealth last for a thousand years, men will still say, 'This was its finest hour.'

SULTAN *salutes* ENOCH *ironically and* ENOCH *salutes him back or else chooses not to salute him and instead tips his hat.*

ENOCH *and* CLEM *go.*

You see how English I was. I could teach most bastard English how to be English.

SULTAN *plays a powerful cricket stroke, dismissing the bowler for four.*

SAEED. English people, who cares. I going back to village, marry *apnee lurkee*. Next year I call her come here.

SULTAN. Saeed, woman wearing *shalwar kameez* in Mirpur is not same woman wearing *shalwar kameez* in Wolverhampton, even identical exact same woman is not same. All change here.

SAEED. Community now. Before, no women, no one praying hardly. Men going *puppley* all that sort of thing. Now women children coming, Sultan uncle. Everything different. Tell *goree* fuck off.

SULTAN. Saeed *putter*, I'm in love.

SAEED. You marry white woman, *lan-dan* finish, uncle. *Tu saan apnay o ya paray?* One of us or one of them?

SULTAN. Some men coming *Inglaan* to work, Saeed. I coming here to be different.

SAEED *exits*.

Scene Eight

Fucking black

December 1992. Wolverhampton. ROSE brings SOFIA to the street where she grew up. But now she's here she sort of hangs back.

ROSE. That's our house.

SOFIA. The street where you grew up always makes you shivery, doesn't it. Physically it's exactly how you remember it but something not right.

ROSE. Like when your gran dies and they show you her corpse.

SOFIA. Big. Big house.

ROSE. We sublet. We had tenants, new immigrants every few months. Two to a room, more.

SOFIA. Was it a lot to take in as a girl?

ROSE. I ignored it. I live in my head mostly.

SOFIA. Is it nice there?

ROSE. No.

SOFIA. Where does Mrs Hughes live?

ROSE. There. Will we go?

SOFIA. What about your mum?

ROSE. We don't speak. I told you.

SOFIA. Why?

ROSE. She's racist.

SOFIA. Is she white?

ROSE. No. Some black cultures – Trinidad, India – the lighter your skin the more attractive you are. She thought I was too black. When your *mother* is racist to you.

SOFIA. Tricky, yes, treacherous, sorry, yes, difficult.

ROSE. One night she came to a school concert (I was taking the parents' coats) and she acted like she didn't know me. She put her coat in the cloakroom like it was a cloak. I thought *I'm your daughter, say hello to me, who are you trying to be*? It was like watching someone in complete denial. In her own bubble.

I spent the evening in the cloakroom alone with the coats; that was the place I became black, I became *fucking* black.

SOFIA. Is *fucking* black is that blacker

ROSE. yes

SOFIA. What is it that *fucking* black adds to blackness?

ROSE. Depth.

SOFIA. She's your enemy really.

ROSE. She wants to tear my skin off.

SOFIA. She's your enemy more than anyone maybe. So if the aim of if what we're trying to do is *talk to people we hate*

ROSE. When I speak she stares at me like I'm talking magpie or something, then *she* says something and I stare at *her*. It's like speaking across a

enchantment.

SOFIA. Our enemies by definition make no sense.

ROSE. She looks down on me with five hundred years of contempt.

SOFIA. Yes but if you don't

ROSE. if I don't

SOFIA. if you don't she's in control of you

ROSE. in control?

SOFIA. what's driving you to drive your car into the river

ROSE. *I'm perfectly capable of driving a car into a river all by myself!*

SOFIA. I just mean

ROSE. When you psychoanalyse people, do you subconsciously want to be slapped.

SOFIA. Seems strange to write about identity and not discuss

ROSE. She's irrational.

SOFIA. That's very close to saying she's not human. She must have reasons.

ROSE. Is there a reason you have more empathy with racists than I have?

SOFIA. I was brought up racist. I'm an immigrant. We're Greek Cypriot.

ROSE. Sofia Nicol?

SOFIA. Nicolou. Came to Britain after the Turks burned out my daddy's business in a riot. We were all racist, Mum, Dad, the whole community, of course we never thought we were racist we thought we'd been robbed. We had a rage against injustice; and a rage against another race. My mother hung herself though we don't know why. She hated my dad for being a taxi driver.

Yes I'm racist. I understand the long hatred. I have to hate who my parents hated a little bit or what kind of daughter would I be. And if *I'm* racist, if my mum and dad are racist, can I object when other people are? Other communities?

ROSE. What age were you? When your mother hung herself?

SOFIA. Thirteen. I was first home from school. She was wearing her coat. Like she was about to go out to the shops and changed her mind.

ROSE. I'm sorry.

SOFIA. I'm sorry I used that.

ROSE. *I'm* sorry I

SOFIA. *I'm* sorry, been a long day, why don't we knock on your mother's door while we're here?

ROSE. She's in hospital. Heart bypass.

SOFIA. Who told you?

ROSE. My brother phones me. We could visit her in hospital. I depress her, you might cheer her up.

SOFIA. Being a snob in hospital is hard work. I remember visiting my mum, after one of her attempts.

We need to talk about petrol money.

Scene Nine

Shropshire

14th April 1968.

ENOCH *enters, having walked five miles of a ridgeway. Tweed suit with waistcoat and country cap, knapsack, stout shoes.* CLEM *enters in corduroy trousers and jacket, gets his food out of a knapsack. Expensive game pie, a bottle of wine.*

ENOCH. The youthfulness, like it's freshly born from the Ice Age. The snow on the tops, ice in the shadows, the hills as fresh as the lambs.

He points below.

Look at that field hedge. Crack willow, alder, blackthorn. A landscape formed by the slow drift of time.

The continuity of English life unbroken over a thousand years, present and visible in that boundary hedge.

The English landscape is a physical record of violent change. The Enclosures, for instance, or the destruction of the countryside since the war. Both men know this.

CLEM. We used to see lapwing around here. Farmers. Intensive farming. Makes you weep.

ENOCH. I would die for Shropshire. Would you?

CLEM. Well look, Enoch, it's not the first thing that occurs. I'm looking forward to a wine that hasn't been made by Marjorie, and some expensive pie.

ENOCH. How is Marjorie?

CLEM. She has standards one rarely meets. When will you make your *last white woman in the street* speech?

ENOCH. I took your advice about timing. Saturday afternoon, AGM of West Midlands CPC. Perfect for Saturday night TV and the Sundays. And I pulled out some quotes from the body of the speech, put them on a front sheet for the convenience of lazy journalists.

CLEM. Glad I could help. Give them anything juicy?

ENOCH. *As I look ahead, I am filled with foreboding; like the Roman, I seem to see 'the River Tiber foaming with much blood'.*

CLEM. Bit obscure isn't it. *Like the Roman*?

ENOCH. Virgil. The prophecy of civil war in Rome.

CLEM *has the beauty and peace of Shropshire around him, and is opening a bottle of wine.*

CLEM. You foresee bloodshed?

ENOCH. Yes.

CLEM. Have you cleared this speech with your colleagues?

ENOCH. No one in the entire Establishment of England is listening to me. *Flectere si nequeo superos, Acheronta movebo.* If I cannot move the powers above, I shall raise hell.

CLEM *gives* ENOCH *a glass of wine.*

CLEM. Talking of hell. The North Wolverhampton Working Men's Club voted to ban coloured people last week. When the result was announced they stamped their feet and roared. Why speak out on behalf of people like that.

ENOCH. Like what?

CLEM. Ignorant, irrational. Almost savage.

ENOCH. Ignorant, irrational, savage. The vocabulary once used by Empire-builders and colonisers to describe the natives, you use about ordinary English working men. You look down on them.

CLEM. No coloured person set foot in the Wolverhampton Working Men's Club *before* the ban; the vote was entirely

ENOCH. They expressed their anger and resentment.

CLEM. Pointless demonstration of

ENOCH. It was a demonstration of their power.

CLEM. They've changed nothing.

ENOCH. They changed the rules of their club, they have done what is in their power to do. They know when they vote in parliamentary elections it will make not the slightest difference; both parties speak loudly against immigration and do nothing to prevent it.

CLEM. The Tory Party is *fiercely* anti-immigrant.

ENOCH. It wishes from time to time to give that impression.

ENOCH *refills his wine glass*.

There's an Irish landlady in Zoar Street, she has eight coloured tenants, the alcoholic Mrs McGinty. When she's drunk she walks up and down the stairs shouting, 'Who are these black so-and-so's, where the dickens did they come from?' The Tory Party is Mrs McGinty in a suit and blue tie. As the party of business it will always encourage immigration, but like Mrs McGinty it will not like to say so in public.

CLEM. Immigrants do bring economic benefits.

ENOCH. Without doubt.

CLEM. They're young, single, they don't incur the same social costs as the indigenous population, they are less ill, less old, less in need of care or pensions.

ENOCH. They are a once-and-for-all gain to the economy. The Treasury, when I was a Minister in the Tory Government, was entirely in their favour. It is true beyond peradventure that immigrants bring economic growth; but on the whole it's employers who reap the benefits and people who pay the costs. *Their* schools are threatened, *their* jobs, their sense of entitlement. When they turn to the Labour Party, does the Labour Party say, 'You are quite right, brothers, Capitalism uses immigrants to keep wages low, and solve short-term labour shortages with no thought for the future consequences.' No, the Labour candidate walks away from their door calling them bigots under his breath. You can only despise your own voters for so long. They will judge you, as you judge them, measure for measure.

CLEM. I don't think we're very far apart, all of us want integration.

ENOCH. Her Majesty's Government and Her Opposition have no other objective or thought.

CLEM. So when racial feelings are running high, is it right to inflame them?

ENOCH. In a democracy people elect a Parliament to speak their mind; if no one does so they will find someone unparliamentary. That is the evil of the present circumstances I wish to turn away.

ENOCH *has finished eating, starts to pack up*.

CLEM. Yes, well, I understand you have obligations and what have you. I would miss our talks.

ENOCH. Our walks. Difficult to make friends. I keep them for life.

CLEM. Yes. You get older, friends disappear. Like lapwing.

Marjorie admires you very much, you know. She admires you enormously.

ENOCH. I have a great fondness for *her*.

CLEM. She clings to you.

ENOCH. Yes.

CLEM. Don't let that deceive you, out of the four of us she's the most principled. I was a conscientious objector during the war, lost my job as a journalist because of the stand I took. She loved me ferociously then.

ENOCH. I know she *disagrees* with my views. Does she disapprove?

CLEM. Yes.

ENOCH. Then you must tell her

Immigration is not a question of right and wrong but of life and death, and something even more important still. The meaning of things. The greatest of human realities the greatest of political realities is the question of identity – who do we think we are? – who am I? – and immigrants present that question in its most dramatic and rawest form. After I made my speech in Walsall, I received hundreds of letters from Black Country folk. I've never had such a response. You know when you're articulating the feelings of the whole people of England. It's what Winston did in the war. You don't call a people into being but in a sense you do. You call to the, you call them out. You give them an identity.

CLEM. I don't see the need.

ENOCH *shoulders his bag*.

ENOCH. Could you and Marjorie babysit the girls? The speech is in The Birmingham Midland Hotel, Pam and I will drive down, drive straight back up. Won't be any later than five.

CLEM. Yes no reason not.

ENOCH. It's been a wonderful friendship.

CLEM. Shall we go?

ENOCH. Yes.

Scene Ten

The Birmingham Speech

20th April 1968. The Midland Hotel, Birmingham.

Watched by the characters in the play, ENOCH *makes a speech to the audience.*

ENOCH. Mr Chairman, ladies and gentlemen.

The supreme function of statesmanship is to provide against preventable evils. In seeking to do so, it encounters obstacles which are deeply rooted in human nature.

One is that by the very order of things such evils are not demonstrable until they have occurred; whence the besetting temptation of all politics to concern itself with the immediate present at the expense of the future.

A week or two ago I fell into conversation with a constituent, a middle-aged, quite ordinary working man employed in one of our nationalised industries.

A decent ordinary fellow Englishman. After a sentence or two about the weather, he suddenly said: 'If I had the money to go, I wouldn't stay in this country. I have three children, all of them been through grammar school and two of them married now, with family. I shan't be satisfied till I have seen them all settled overseas. In this country in fifteen or twenty years' time the black man will have the whip hand over the white man.'

I can already hear the chorus of execration. How dare I say such a horrible thing? How dare I stir up trouble and inflame feelings by repeating such a conversation?

My answer is that I do not have the right not to do so.

What he is saying, thousands and hundreds of thousands are saying and thinking – not throughout Great Britain, perhaps, but in the areas that are already undergoing the total transformation to which there is no parallel in a thousand years of English history.

In fifteen or twenty years, on present trends, there will be in this country three and a half million Commonwealth immigrants and their descendants. Of course, it will not be evenly distributed from Margate to Aberystwyth and from Penzance to Aberdeen. Whole towns and parts of towns across England will be occupied by sections of the immigrant and immigrant-descended population.

Those whom the gods wish to destroy, they first make mad. We must be mad, literally mad, as a nation to be permitting the annual inflow of some fifty thousand dependents, who are for the most part the material of the future growth of the immigrant-descended population. It is like watching a nation busily engaged in heaping up its own funeral pyre.

There could be no grosser misconception of the realities than is entertained by those who vociferously demand legislation as they call it 'against discrimination'. They have got it exactly and diametrically wrong. The discrimination and the deprivation, the sense of alarm and of resentment, lies not with the immigrant population but with those among whom they have come and are still coming.

While, to the immigrant, entry to this country was admission to privileges and opportunities eagerly sought, the impact upon the existing population was very different. For reasons which they could not comprehend, they found themselves made strangers in their own country.

They found their wives unable to obtain hospital beds in childbirth, their children unable to obtain school places, their homes and neighbourhoods changed beyond recognition; they began to hear, as time went by, more and more voices which told them that they were now the unwanted.

The sense of being a persecuted minority which is growing among ordinary English people in the areas of the country which are affected is something that those without direct experience can hardly imagine.

I am going to allow just one of those hundreds of people to speak for me:

Eight years ago in a respectable street in Wolverhampton a house was sold to a Negro. Now only one white lives there. This is her story. She lost her husband in the war. So she turned her seven-roomed house, her only asset, into a boarding house. She worked hard, paid off her mortgage and began to put something by for her old age. Then the immigrants moved in. With growing fear, she saw one house after another taken over. The quiet street became a place of noise and confusion.

She is becoming afraid to go out. Windows are broken. She finds excreta pushed through her letter box. When she goes to the shops, she is followed by children, charming, wide-grinning picaninnies. They cannot speak English, but one word they know. 'Racialist', they chant.

The other dangerous delusion from which those who are wilfully or otherwise blind to realities suffer, is summed up in the word 'integration'.

Now, at all times, where there are marked physical differences, especially of colour, integration is difficult though, over a period, not impossible. There are among the Commonwealth immigrants who have come to live here in the last fifteen years or so, many thousands whose wish and purpose is to be integrated and whose every thought and endeavour is bent in that direction.

But to imagine that such a thing enters the heads of a great and growing majority of immigrants and their descendants is a ludicrous misconception, and a dangerous one.

Now we are seeing the growth of positive forces acting against integration, of vested interests in the preservation and sharpening of racial and religious differences, with a view to the exercise of actual domination, first over fellow-immigrants and then over the rest of the population. The words I am about to use are not mine, but those of a Labour Member of Parliament who is a minister in the present Labour Government:

'The Sikh communities' campaign to wear their turbans while working on British buses is much to be regretted. Working in Britain, particularly in the public services, they should be prepared to accept the terms and conditions of their employment. To claim special communal rights leads to a dangerous fragmentation within society. This communalism is a canker; whether practised by one colour or another it is to be strongly condemned.'

As I look ahead, I am filled with foreboding; like the Roman, I seem to see the River Tiber foaming with much blood.

Race riots, that tragic and intractable phenomenon which we watch with horror on the other side of the Atlantic is coming upon us here by our own volition and our own neglect. Indeed, it has all but come. Only resolute and urgent action will avert it even now. Whether there will be the public will to demand and obtain that action, I do not know. All I know is that to see, and not to speak, would be the great betrayal.

Scene Eleven

Greek

Wolverhampton. 20th April 1968.

CLEM *in gardening clothes or tending his bees*. MARJORIE *comes out into the garden. She has a copy of the speech, an advanced copy* ENOCH *has sent to her newspaper editor husband.*

CLEM. Have they picked up the girls yet?

MARJORIE. No.

CLEM. Oh. They're late.

MARJORIE. You helped him. Do I need to say it twice? You helped him.

CLEM. You asked me.

MARJORIE. We needed them. We clung to them, like children crying not to be sent to bed. The humiliation. How can I step outside my door like this.

CLEM. Like what?

MARJORIE. As me!

Sunday tomorrow, the looks we'll get at meeting for worship.

CLEM. We've come through worse. The isolation during the war. Remember people did to us.

MARJORIE. Tar under my nail for weeks.

CLEM. The smell. Sweet. Clingy.

MARJORIE. Young then. Harder now.

CLEM. I don't see why we

MARJORIE. Oh for crying out loud I loved you then.

This is a bullet.

CLEM. Oh dear. The verb *to love* when used in the past tense.

ENOCH *and* PAMELA *enter.*

PAMELA. Sorry we're late.

ENOCH. Caught up in football traffic on the way back.

PAMELA. How were the girls?

MARJORIE. I read your speech.

PAMELA. Yes, it's a corker, isn't it.

MARJORIE. The girls are upstairs playing. You can shout them down.

PAMELA. Yes. Righto.

MARJORIE. We won't be seeing each other for a very long time.

PAMELA. Oh. I see.

ENOCH. We are breaking up.

MARJORIE. I thought the world of you, Enoch. *Picaninnies?* How could you use such a word?

ENOCH. I didn't. I was quoting a letter a woman sent me.

MARJORIE. Why did you quote an idiot? She says the picaninnies cannot speak English. What does she imagine they speak, Zulu? Get out.

ENOCH. As Pericles says in his great speech φερειν χρη τα τε δαιμονια αναγχαιως I will bear what the gods send with resignation.

MARJORIE's reaction is Greek in intensity. A hiss of contempt and seething anger. The other three remain middle-class and masked.

The POWELLS *exit, leaving the* JONESES *alone.*

MARJORIE. This is the end; you know that, don't you?

She's talking about their marriage. They might not divorce but it's over.

ACT TWO

Scene One

'Enoch Powell'

December 1992. ENOCH *in his usual three-piece suit. He is eighty. He walks on. Ten metres is an epic journey.*

DR SHARMA, *in his twenties, comes in, sets up markers.*

DR SHARMA. Yes, good good good, so Mr Powell I want to look at how you walk.

ENOCH *looks back at the epic journey he has made.*

ENOCH. If you'd been here when I arrived.

DR SHARMA. Look at stride time, stride length.

ENOCH. You assessed my walking prowess at our previous consultation.

DR SHARMA. Parkinson's is a progressive illness, want to measure the deterioration.

DR SHARMA *watches* ENOCH *walk and does his assessment.*

Do you have trouble with your balance?

ENOCH. Yes.

DR SHARMA. Do you sometimes fall over?

ENOCH. Yes.

DR SHARMA Do you have difficulty with stairs?

ENOCH. I understand the concept.

DR SHARMA. Do you sometimes freeze?

ENOCH. Freeze?

DR SHARMA. When you walk, do you sometimes freeze, unable to move.

ENOCH. No.

DR SHARMA. Are you drooling yet?

ENOCH. No.

DR SHARMA. Are you incontinent yet?

ENOCH. I was once a power in the land, said Powell rather defiantly.

DR SHARMA. How little sleep are you getting?

ENOCH. Death appears ever more attractive.

DR SHARMA. Are you having hallucinations yet? Some patients have a sense of a shadow at their shoulder.

ENOCH. There was a severed head on the pillow beside me this morning.

DR SHARMA. Good. And what is your mental condition. I am wondering for example your knowledge of current affairs. Who is the Prime Minister?

ENOCH. It is of no consequence. He's a nobody.

DR SHARMA. Have you forgotten?

ENOCH. It is too painful to remember.

DR SHARMA. How do you pass the time?

ENOCH. I tender advice to the Sovereign.

DR SHARMA.How would you describe arrogance?

ENOCH. Brilliantly.

> DR SHARMA *puts his pen down*.

DR SHARMA. Is there anything you'd like to ask me?

> Or say?

> You're staring at me.

ENOCH. I used to be Enoch Powell.

DR SHARMA. Used to be?

> ENOCH *begins to shake – which makes him embarrassed and annoyed and shake even worse.*

ENOCH. This tremor.

DR SHARMA. A tremor is perfectly normal symptom of Parkinson's.

ENOCH (*shaking increases throughout*). My fellow countrymen invite me to speak on the great issues of the day and if I am holding notes the tremor can all too plainly be seen. We have a word for an argument '*shaky*', it is not a word you wish to see forming in the mind of your audience as you speak. Shaking beyond one's power to cause or control is a great lesson in humility but when it happens to me all I can think is

> this is not who I am, this is not who I am, this is not who I am, this is not who I am.

> *The tremor ends.*

> Is there a trick?

DR SHARMA. A trick?

ENOCH. I invited him to a small church in Gloucestershire.

DR SHARMA. Invited who?

ENOCH. A former friend. We have one chance to understand each other and be reconciled. I wish *not* to be distracted by a tremor and anxiety often sets it in motion.

DR SHARMA. Be yourself, Mr Powell, be yourself.

Scene Two

The Changeling

December 1992.

The sound of a helicopter grows.

An old woman on a rooftop. GRACE MAHMOOD, *formerly Grace Hughes. She walks to the edge of the rooftop, realises she has nowhere to go. The helicopter passes over her, lights her. She guards herself against the noise and updraft. When it passes, she shakes her fist at it. She's a determined soul.*

SULTAN *comes out on to the roof, followed by* ROSE *and* SOFIA.

SULTAN. What you doing, Grace, love, this is roof of fucking hospital.

GRACE. Do you mind not calling me *love*?

SULTAN. It's me, it's Sultan, your husband.

GRACE. I'm a widow. I'm a war widow.

SULTAN. That your first husband, I'm second husband.

GRACE. Never met you afore my whole life.

SULTAN. What are you talking about, we are visiting Mrs fucking Cruickshank in hospital, we are bumping into Mrs fucking Cruickshank daughter Rose. I say let's go home and watch some telly welly and all of a sudden disabloodypear.

GRACE. I'm running away from you, you ghost.

SULTAN (*to* ROSE *and* SOFIA). See how she denies me, this is what I'm telling you.

GRACE. You're a shadow that's what you are.

SULTAN. Two three months you are denying me, I should tear you to pieces with my bare hands. Ya Allah, what do I do to persuade you I'm your husband? I give you my love, my will

He empties his pockets, takes off his parka.

here, take my wallet, keys, credit card, take the bloody
smash I have. Take my clothes, bloody everything. I am
telling you, this is tragedy of brown people and white people,
you want to *fuck* us we want to *be* you.

GRACE. You're all after summat.

ROSE. Mrs Hughes, do you remember me?

SULTAN. Why she remember *you*, I'm her husband.

ROSE. I'm Rose, Rose Cruickshank.

GRACE. Keep away from me.

ROSE. My mother's Mrs Cruickshank, we were neighbours.

SOFIA. Rose, you're scaring her.

ROSE. I'm trying to help.

SOFIA. Don't push her.

ROSE. I'm not pushing her.

SOFIA. Can we all just go inside.

ROSE. I'm trying to have a conversation. I'm just telling her
who I am.

GRACE. I know who you are. You spat all over me in the street,
she spat all over me when she were a kid. Were a whole gang
of 'em round me, nignogs like. Pulled my hair, had a kick at
me, told me to eff off I weren't wanted.

ROSE. Nignogs? I feel bad questioning your memory
questioning her memory in the circum

GRACE. You don't forget people who spit at you.

ROSE. accusation made by a woman that's climbed on to the
roof of a five-storey building sadly

GRACE (*talking over 'sadly'*). I told your mam, I told Mrs
Cruickshank, she were mortified, said she hated to see her
daughter behavin like a black.

ROSE. What to say. I'm lost.

SERGEANT SHERGAR *enters. He's a turban-wearing Sikh policeman.*

SERGEANT SHERGAR. They said there was a woman on the rooftop in distress.

SOFIA. You've got a choice of three.

That's her there, officer.

SERGEANT SHERGAR. Can I ask you what's wrong, love?

GRACE. Running away from that thing.

SULTAN. I am idiot fucking husband.

GRACE. All day every day, every time I turn around, gets into bed with me and all. He even looks like my husband. Sounds like him and all.

SERGEANT SHERGAR. What's your name, love?

GRACE. Grace Hughes.

SERGEANT SHERGAR. How'd you end up on this roof?

GRACE. Going to Much Wenlock. Shropshire lass I am.

SERGEANT SHERGAR. A454 you want, why don't you come with me, love, till you get your bearings.

GRACE. You arresting me? She's the one you wunna take.

SERGEANT SHERGAR (*humouring* GRACE). Oh, what's she done then?

GRACE. She spat at me.

SERGEANT SHERGAR. When was this then?

GRACE. I don't know the date, do I. I were coming home after the game.

SERGEANT SHERGAR. What game?

GRACE. Wolves – Liverpool.

ROSE. Can someone help her away.

SERGEANT SHERGAR (*to* GRACE). Come on, babs, let's get
a cuppa tea. Wolves lost today, the fans got faces on them
like bulldogs lickin piss off a thistle. So I'll take you to a caff
I go to when I want to wag it for a bit.

GRACE *goes to* SERGEANT SHERGAR.

SULTAN (*Mirpuri*). Grace. You are my beloved. What am
I without you?

GRACE (*Mirpuri*). You fool, go and ask someone.

SERGEANT SHERGAR (*to* SULTAN). Phone us later, alright?

SERGEANT SHERGAR *exits with* GRACE.

SULTAN *is metaphysically lost*.

SULTAN. where is she? she has gone some country she is only
one who lives there.

ROSE. confusing, painful

SOFIA. *freezing*, can we get down off this roof

SULTAN (*rejecting this offer*). I'm saying goodbye!

ROSE. saying goodbye

SULTAN. my wife is deserting me in dribs and fucking drabs!

ROSE. she's not who she was, is she

SULTAN. we had silver anniversary in bloody Tenerife!

last two three months she don't recognise me, treat me like a
Paki. you have a story in your head, your identity and all
that, who you are and all this, one day someone rewrite you

ROSE. one day someone rewrites you

SULTAN. one day things stop making sense

ROSE. I laughed when she accused me of spitting.

She didn't.

SULTAN. Saeed see the spitting incident, you remember Saeed?

ROSE. Saeed, yes I remember Saeed

SULTAN. he tell you everything, who he saw and all that, he
tell you exactly.

ROSE. did he describe the incident to you?

SULTAN. he tell me word for word. I take you to see him
tomorrow

ROSE. good. yes.

SULTAN. good. meanwhile too freezing cold to stand here
crying from the fucking rooftop

SULTAN *exits*.

SOFIA. identity. keeps coming unfixed. by the time you've
described today it's tomorrow

ROSE. yeah

ROSE *looks over the edge of the building*.

SOFIA. you okay?

ROSE. madwoman on a rooftop

SOFIA. you're not *mad*

ROSE. I meant her.

the closest to real life *most* radical left-wing academics get
is the black lady that serves them in the faculty-building
cafeteria. I get attacked by a demented racist on a hospital
rooftop.

even our memories are prejudiced.

SOFIA. what way?

ROSE. like poor Mrs Hughes, we edit the story of our lives. we
snip things out or make things up

SOFIA. yes. you sure you want to meet Saeed?

ROSE. yes

SOFIA. story's not complete till we see things from everyone's
perspective.

ROSE. yes

SOFIA. right. Saeed tomorrow. Enoch Powell on Monday

ROSE. right

>*They exit.*

Scene Three

What Shadows

December 1992.

Hailes Church, Gloucestershire. A back wall, on which we see the shadow of a giant St Christopher carrying the shadow of an infant Christ on his shoulder. The shadow of a medieval wall painting once hidden beneath a Reformation whitewash. CLEM *enters. He's seventy-seven now but pretty fit.*

ENOCH. What shadows we are. What shadows we pursue.

>ENOCH *has been waiting.*

CLEM. Twelfth century.

ENOCH. Early English windows added later. All the murals of saints would have been whitewashed over during the Reformation, of course. Violent fearful times, the kings and queens of England still deciding which religion the country should be. Shakespeare was baptised Protestant, his older sister Catholic. His father oversaw the whitewashing of the Stratford Guild church, the erasure of Catholic images. All over England the people stopped going to church, there was a great silent refusal. They did not recognise the churches they had grown up in.

CLEM. Seems unlikely we could know what people *felt* all those years ago.

ENOCH. We can infer from Acts of Parliament. The 1552 Act
  of Uniformity complained the people *do wilfully and
  damnably abstain and refuse to come to their parish church.*
  In spite of fines and worse.

CLEM. Peace now. A sense of presence. Kindness.

ENOCH. I was sorry to hear the news about Marjorie.

CLEM. Yes, this time last year.

ENOCH. Did she ever forgive me?

CLEM. No.

ENOCH. Did you?

CLEM. In the aftermath of the speech it was difficult for
  prominent nigger-lovers like me, bricks through our living-
  room window, that sort of thing. I swept up the broken glass
  thinking *I helped Enoch inspire the moron who did this.*

ENOCH. You created a monster.

CLEM. I've been fighting it ever since.

ENOCH. I read the book you wrote for the Commission on
  Racial Equality about race and the media. You condemned
  my manipulation of the press. About the part you played you
  were entirely silent. Did you ever tell your black friends?

CLEM. No. There was no necessity.

ENOCH. You are a very lonely furrow.

CLEM. You were a dirty secret.

   PAMELA *enters, carrying a bag full of letters.*

PAMELA. Clem. You've weathered *very* well.

CLEM. Thank you.

PAMELA. I was sorry to hear about Marjorie.

CLEM. She said you met up.

PAMELA. We both had a bit of a cry.

CLEM. It's good you and Marjorie at least. I'm glad you two.

PAMELA. We were great friends the four of us. When Enoch and Marjorie got going, goodness, the conversation the *allusions*, way above us poor mortals.

CLEM. You two were an oasis.

PAMELA. Oasis, gosh.

CLEM. For Marjorie, yes. Oh yes. Life was very stony without you. Then luckily I got sacked, not being in tune with my readership, too liberal, too wet. When I told Marjorie the news she looked me up and down like I'd pulled my moral socks up.

PAMELA. It's lovely to see you. Enoch and I lost a lot of friends after his speech.

ENOCH. Like fleas deserting a sinking rat.

PAMELA. Of course friends in your own Party are never really your friends.

I brought some of the letters Enoch received after his speech. Thirty thousand in two days, a hundred thousand in the end, Royal Mail vans stuffed full of them. Here, Enoch, read one.

He takes at random a letter from the bag she has brought.

ENOCH. *Thank God someone has spoken for the working classes of England who fought a World War to enable their children to live a better life. We sweated and toiled and shed rivers of blood as you know and when victory was ours and the enemy was defeated we got our National Health and decent housing and welfare state and now the traitor politicians have handed the things we fought for to the immigrants, the hordes of black locusts*

CLEM. *Black locusts*. You couldn't make it up.

ENOCH. The imagery people use. Noise dirt rats diseases plague, like the chorus of a Greek tragedy casting round for an answer to the riddle that has entered their lives.

CLEM. You their prophet, did you whisper the words that would have delivered them?

ENOCH. I gave them a sense of identity they were crying out for.

CLEM. And now even our flag is divisive, it's the flag of *white racist* England.

ENOCH. I held up a mirror.

CLEM. It smashed into a million fragments. The pieces lodged in our eyes.

ENOCH. I invited you here so we might be reconciled.

There's a desire to heal the breach but how?

CLEM. There's been a breach.

ENOCH. There is division.

CLEM. How do we talk to each other?

ENOCH. Is the fault all on one side?

We have just had the business with Salman Rushdie, his book burned in Bradford, Muslim fundamentalists accusing him of blasphemy, demanding the book be pulped, ayatollahs issuing a *fatwa* authorising and encouraging Muslims to execute the author. The *fatwa* was described as *barbarian* even by the left-wing playwright Harold Pinter.

CLEM. Yes, every liberal in the country suddenly went racist. *Barbarian*. Liberals love immigrants until they turn out to be fundamentally *different*.

ENOCH. To share an identity with someone it is necessary not that you agree with his opinions but that you agree which century it is; the religion of a Muslim is medieval in its unreason, its intolerance of free speech and of satire.

CLEM. You don't mean a Muslim, you mean a Muslim fundamentalist.

ENOCH. Very well, a Muslim fundamentalist.

CLEM. England was fundamentalist once. Look at this church. In every little village of rural England, fundamentalist Protestants methodically destroyed the art of a civilisation, erased every trace of opposition, in the same way today we try to erase each other in argument.

The English in these churches were obliged to worship in whatever way their king did; there was a monoculture. When dissenters like we Quakers met to pray in silence we were arrested for riot, attacked on the streets with clubs like a plague of frogs. Then came the 1689 Act of Toleration, we were allowed.

It always surprises me the suspicion with which we treat the word *multicultural* as if it's a recent arrival from abroad and ought to be held in a detention centre pending investigation. The concept is as English as tea, older than your house or anything you have in your possession, it predates our roads and the entire fabric of England. It was a decision we took three hundred years ago, Act of Toleration, not to define Englishness, not to nationalise it, but to tolerate people whose beliefs are fundamentally different from our own. Multiculturalism's not about being nice, it's what the country's built of.

ENOCH. There is a difficulty, however. How can a multicultural country tolerate fundamentalists?

Silence.

PAMELA. I'll go. I'll wait outside.

She goes.

CLEM. How do we speak across the divide?

ENOCH. Two old men. Dead soon.

Silence.

CLEM. Conscientious objectors, we I was called un-English during the war. You go about your business doing your work. It's like being exiled in your own country.

ENOCH. It was hard not to think of you as traitors.

Silence.

CLEM. And what I mean to say is, one's identity one's
nationality

I struggle.

The war widow in your speech

Ethel my mother Ethel was a war widow. Never spoke about
my father, told me not to ask to ask about him. I remember
that, being scolded, she cut him out of her wedding album.
Furious with him for dying.

21st Battalion Middlesex Regiment. I found out after Ethel
died. Killed the battle of Cambrai, the First War, a Sikh
cavalry regiment charged the German tanks to protect their
retreat. People sometimes say their father was very distant,
mine was non-existent and Ethel, you remember, wrapped
herself around me *like ivy*. When we had our boys I wanted
more than anything to be close to them. But, you know

no idea how.

and in a way the father I had the mother I had, that's why
friends with you, you see. I shared your thirst for solitude.

Silence.

ENOCH. My raging thirst for solitude.

CLEM. In the end, if you live long enough, you get all the
solitude in the world.

They sit there in solitude. In tears.

Scene Four

The World Turned Upside Down

SAEED *has been cleaning his car. He has a hoover or a bucket or cleaning materials.*

SULTAN *arrives, with* ROSE *and* SOFIA.

SULTAN. *salaam alaikum*

SAEED. *walaikum salaam.*

They embrace.

SULTAN. remember Mrs Cruickshank daughter Rose?

SAEED. Mrs Cruickshank's daughter Rose

ROSE. you recognise me?

SAEED. recognise recognise

ROSE. I'm a historian now, this is my colleague, Sofia

SAEED. you can write my history. twenty-five years ago, I work rolling*mill*foundry. three children now. did electronics night school, got better job.

He gives her a chance to write this down but she doesn't.

you can write it down you wish

ROSE/SOFIA. Yes / yes, of course

SULTAN. *cuppa chah* would be nice

SAEED. I'm sorry, you see my wife

I'm dying you see, I have brain cancer isn't it. you are coming at very bad time

SULTAN. who is dying. nobody is dying.

SAEED. my wife very angry

SULTAN. twenty years younger than me

SAEED. stress and everything, losing her hair

been good to me, my car, stood me in good stead. power steering power windows, fully serviced, still has manual everything. only three thousand miles on clock. nice *family* car, will give it to Mina. good girl, I always know she won't do anything wrong.

SULTAN. you, you bastard, you can't tell me you're dying prepare me on the phone? I come here and you bastard apologise you are dying?

He switches to stereotypical Asian accent.

goodness gracious me I am having brain cancer

SAEED. surprising

surprised

SULTAN. will they bury you back in the village?

SAEED. *nay. dil heh Pakistan mein* but Pakistan too far for children to visit the old man's grave. here now. all of us here now.

I invite you for tea but my wife is angry you see

ROSE. of course of course of course, I complete I mean totally, I can't even imagine

SAEED. I don't know how to apologise

ROSE. don't don't don't

SULTAN. why we are here, the day the black kids are spitting at Grace before she became my wife

SAEED. yes

ROSE. you saw it?

SAEED. long long time ago

ROSE. whatever you do or don't remember

SAEED. they kicking pushing spitting on her, calling her names. she is white with fear, white as a root.

ROSE. who did, Saeed sahib, who spat on her?

SAEED. five six seven kids

ROSE. did you recognise them?

SAEED. recognise, yes.

ROSE. did you see *me*?

SAEED. see you yes.

ROSE. how can you be sure?

SAEED. you walk past me like you done nothing wrong but
you see you have spit in your hair. I say, *Rose you have spit
in your hair*.

Unconsciously ROSE *puts her hand to her hair.*

you look guilty as everything, put your hand to your head
and say *Is it spitting with rain?* is grey day but dry dry. no
rain interruptions all day.

…

…

SOFIA. Rose is going to meet Enoch Powell. anything you
want to say to him?

SAEED. Enoch Powell. no.

ROSE. after his speech, was there more racism, Saeed sahib,
were there more attacks for instance (don't want to influence
you) more attacks on Asians?

SAEED. more attacks, yes

ROSE. anything else you want to say?

SAEED. I've had beautiful life. in village we work before
school. you want to relieve yourself you go out to field and
do it. now Mina say Daddy I'm going out for a curry with
the girls! she say to me Daddy you know what I hate about
Ramzan I don't lose any fucking weight.

coming to *vilayit* on cruise ship

SULTAN. sailors on cruise ship from his village, they smuggle
him aboard

SAEED. cruise ship I see things I never see. carpets
    runningwater ice cream. I get off boat long time ago but still
    sailing sailing

Pause.

SOFIA. yes. you have two lives, hard to join them up.

SULTAN (*Mirpuri*). Saeed, I am losing Grace, losing my mind.
    you won't give me cuppa chah shah?

SAEED (*Mirpuri*). and them as well?

SULTAN (*Mirpuri*). no. not them.

SAEED (*to* ROSE). bye, Rose. here is pieceofadvice. Nissan
    Sunny good family car.

ROSE. thank you Sultan, thank you Saeed, I appreciate it.

SULTAN *and* SAEED *exit.*

strange. mysterious. don't know whether to believe him or not

SOFIA. you do

ROSE. I do?

SOFIA. you do believe him. when he was telling the story of
    you as a girl you put your hand to your head like a girl with
    spit in her hair. like you remembered.

The shame hits her.

ROSE. I'm a racist? I stood up at conferences on post-
    colonialism, addressed them from the castle of my skin! in the
    pub afterwards, shouted other academics down in arguments,
    not shout, just was a teensy bit more clever than the others,
    more right. *I spat at a white woman.* How can I stand in front
    of my students and *teach*?

SOFIA. teach you can be mistaken

ROSE (*exploding with fury and shame*). oh for jesus' sake Sofia
    don't fucking act like you're right. What about the structural
    racism of the police, the deaths in custody, the racism of
    immigration policy, the sense of exclusion black kids feel.

I am fucking black and I'm not going to betray black people
by standing in front of white students and *confessing*, tearing
myself to pieces, so you can say Look, we're *all* racist. So
you can say you were right all along.

SOFIA. Never seen anything more human.

ROSE. I've been stripped of my dignity.

SOFIA. Never felt closer to you.

ROSE. I'm as naked as a slave for sale.

SOFIA. When I was at Oxford I thought no one could touch me.
The cleverest woman in England. You feel such a fool. Your
husband's been fucking students behind your back. For
example. Such a cliché. The pain, and then of course it's
your job as an intellectual *to know more than*, to know more
than everyone else. It's your identity. So when you know
less, when you're exposed. You stand there. The world goes
on spinning.

ROSE. The madwoman on the rooftop knew more about me
than I did.

SOFIA. I knew less than everyone.

ROSE. I knew less than me.

SOFIA. It's humiliating.

ROSE. I wouldn't touch me with a shitty stick.

SOFIA. Yes, you don't want anyone to see you, you feel

ROSE. for christ's sake, Sofia, *I spat at an old lady*. We're
untouchable.

SOFIA. You said *we*. *We're* untouchable.

ROSE. you mean, you and me we're

SOFIA. we're

ROSE. us

SOFIA. we've seen each other's shadow side.

The stuff we'd rather not admit.

ROSE. My mum *stole* my shadow.

SOFIA. In what sense?

ROSE. When I was little. She stole my I don't know.

SOFIA. *My* mum. I just thought she was a snob. Then she killed herself and became a mystery.

ROSE. You never found out why?

SOFIA. Afterwards, when we talked, my sisters and me, we all knew various different tiny bits and pieces about her. And we'd argue over who knew most. But in the vastness of our ignorance...

ROSE. Yes. You were equal.

SOFIA. I suppose so, yes.

ROSE. Listen, nobody else needs to know about all this

SOFIA. no.

ROSE. don't feel it's necessary

SOFIA. of course! if you don't

ROSE. no. I don't.

SOFIA. of course. it opens up a conversation though doesn't it.

ROSE. conversation?

SOFIA. with yourself. I mean that's what identity is really isn't it, an ongoing conversation with yourself and the people around you

ROSE. yes. around. yes. let's get Enoch Powell out of the way first. I don't want all this clouding my head when I'm talking to Powell.

Scene Five

A Vast Inhospitable Landscape

December 1992. Three in the morning.

ENOCH POWELL, *in dressing gown, is going from his bedroom to his study. He passes a hat-stand, so decides to put on his hat. This is an extremely difficult task. But he manages it.*

CLEM *enters, dressed for a hill walk. He's coming back to look for* MARJORIE.

CLEM. Marjorie?

MARJORIE *enters, barefoot, with her boots around her neck.*

You're miles behind.

MARJORIE. I took my boots off. I'm doing it barefoot.

CLEM. Why?

MARJORIE. I'm being pagan.

CLEM. Your feet are cut to ribbons.

MARJORIE. Good.

CLEM. Stony path to the top.

CLEM *exits.* MARJORIE *follows.*

PAMELA *enters in dressing gown.*

PAMELA. Enoch. What are you doing?

ENOCH. I'm crossing a vast inhospitable landscape.

PAMELA. In search of what?

ENOCH. The Milner Holland Committee Report on Housing, 1965. I'm meeting the Oxford academic today.

PAMELA. The picanninny?

ENOCH. She asked to record the interview, I said she can.

PAMELA. I hope you don't underestimate how clever she is.

ENOCH. It is not to be conjectured she is my intellectual equal.

PAMELA. She has the advantage of youth, the study's that way.

The opposite direction to the one in which ENOCH *has been making his epic journey.*

ENOCH. This reminds me. I should like to rehearse my funeral.

PAMELA. You'll be a corpse, Enoch, what can go wrong. Why don't I phone and put her off.

ENOCH. No. I should like to be Enoch Powell again.

PAMELA. She wants a story, Enoch. And when she tells that story, who is the audience likely to sympathise with, a young black woman or the old man who called her a name.

ENOCH. I will not unsay anything I've said.

PAMELA. Will that increase the sympathy?

ENOCH. I held up a mirror to England.

PAMELA. I agree.

ENOCH. I was right.

PAMELA. Yes.

ENOCH. Every word I said has been borne out by events.

PAMELA. So why meet her, what have you got to say you haven't said?

He has to bring out something he's been withholding.

ENOCH. It's of no use to be right today, if in the end I'm proven to be wrong. Change changing changes.

PAMELA (*exiting*). I'll get you the Milner Holland Report.

ENOCH. I argue because I must. There is no taste in nothing.

PAMELA *has exited.*

CLEM *enters in hill-walking gear, exactly as before.*

CLEM. Marjorie?

MARJORIE enters, with boots around her neck as before.

You're miles behind.

MARJORIE. I took my boots off. I'm doing it barefoot.

CLEM. Why?

MARJORIE. I'm being pagan.

CLEM. Your feet are cut to ribbons.

MARJORIE. Good.

CLEM. Let me help you.

He goes to help her put her boots on.

ENOCH. You accuse me of creating division.

The division is none of my doing. In a utopian universe where housing was affordable and jobs plentiful, where all believed themselves heard and understood, no community would resent any other community. Alas, *non semper Saturnalia erunt*. In real life people wish to live happily ever after and are looking for someone to blame.

CLEM (*to* MARJORIE). How's that?

MARJORIE stands up in her boots.

MARJORIE (*to* CLEM). Agony.

CLEM (*to* MARJORIE). I've had a miserable life too, if that's any consolation.

Scene Six

Like Apes

Warwick Cemetery, December 1992.

Crows. ROSE *enters and sets up her microphone.*

SOFIA *enters.*

ROSE. Say something.

> *She wants to test if the recorder's working.*

SOFIA. Why did he suggest a cemetery?

ROSE. He sleeps here, I imagine.

SOFIA. Graveyard's appropriate place to lay things to rest.

ROSE. Or drive a stake through his heart.

SOFIA. Talk about demonising someone.

ROSE. When we were kids, he *was* a demon. After that speech, white kids used to say *Enoch will get you lot*. Or *Knock knock, it's Enoch*. Immigrants were attacked, schools, work, streets. He needs to hear that.

SOFIA. I thought we'd come looking for common ground.

ROSE. In the end it's about right and wrong.

SOFIA. The problem with right and wrong is: if I'm right, you're wrong. Why bother talking? And with all the diversity we have, the proliferating diversity of hatreds. The feminist and the Muslim. The Left and the white working-class. The problem of England is how to survive the hatreds, sharing an island with people we loathe.

ROSE. We educate them.

SOFIA. Because we *know more than*?

ROSE. Sometimes we do know more than, yes.

SOFIA. Knowledge. What do I know? One of my husband's ( )

*The brackets indicate words she can't bring herself to say.
The kindest words would be 'One of my husband's series of
students'.*

used to babysit our girls. And you. Don't make me remind
you.

ROSE. Remind me of what?

SOFIA. The madwoman on the rooftop.

ROSE. He's the arch enemy.

SOFIA. You and I were enemies. You took my job. You took
years. And I'm saying to you. Other people. They might live
in profound ignorance. They might be bigots. But they know
what it's like to be them.

ROSE *sees* ENOCH *offstage*.

ROSE. He's arrived. In his pre-war three-piece suit. Waistcoat
and fob watch. Living in some mythical past.

SOFIA. He has his truth.

ROSE. Unicorns *shit* more truth.

SOFIA. Rose, you came to my beach. I joined you. Now what?
A manual, you said.

ROSE. Yes but what does that mean?

SOFIA. Show us. Here. Now. Get something on tape we can
use. A method for talking to people we hate. A rhetorical
framework. Let's talk about identity as if it's a matter of life
and death, because it is. My mum's still hanging there. Still
hanging. Like an exclamation mark. Like a scream. Make it
mean something.

SOFIA *exits*. ENOCH *enters*.

ROSE. How much would you say you know about England?

ENOCH. Well, I wrote a history of it.

ROSE. Yes. In your 'Rivers of Blood' speech

ENOCH. I call it the Birmingham speech

ROSE. you talked about the immigration of the 1950s and 1960s.

ENOCH. Yes, the scale of the immigration. The sense of being invaded.

ROSE. Was there no sense of invasion in 1066?

ENOCH. The Normans were not as numerous.

ROSE. They built a thousand castles.

ENOCH. One ruling class replaced another. The people might have shrugged and thought *what's the difference*.

ROSE. Give me a year.

ENOCH. 1709.

ROSE. The entire East End of London spoke French. Textile workers. Another.

ENOCH. 1376.

ROSE. Bristol, Norwich, Guildford. Every nook and cranny of England, Somerset, Devon. Overrun by blue nails from Flanders, manufacturing cotton from wool. They created the wealth which built the wool churches.

ENOCH. I was making a speech to my countrymen. When an ordinary English man or woman dwells with pride on a thousand years of English history their minds reach as far back as their nan.

ROSE. There were larger migrations in your lifetime. Before us were the Jews. More of them than us. And before the Jews the Irish, even larger. Riots and pitched battles all over the shop. Moorfields London, Juvenal Street Liverpool, hundreds dead, rivers of blood. Then we come along. As a statesman (I give you the character you give yourself) as a statesman speaking to his people you might have said *We have been here many times before. Let's look at the numerous parallels in our history to see how the problems were overcome.*

ENOCH. The Irish were not as a culture so alien.

ROSE. The Church of Scotland demanded their deportation on the grounds they were an inferior race. Camden, Sparkhill, the Gorbals, living in separate communities like Pakistanis now. We were a total transformation to which there is no parallel in a thousand years of English history only if you meant a transformation in colour.

ENOCH. You are British but you will never be English. We do not share a history.

ROSE. How can we, you don't know any.

ENOCH. Everything depends on the first person plural. In this last generation the word *we* has become a ghost, the white people of England look at once familiar parts of Bradford or Leicester and see clothes and costumes entirely unfamiliar to them. The immigrants bulldozed not the bombed ruins of post-war England but the meaning of things.

ROSE. We confused you.

ENOCH. You are able to understand the shock and dislocation of the immigrants but not the shock and dislocation of the people among whom they came.

ROSE. When I was six, we left my dad. Went to Wolverhampton. Three days trawling around in our Hillman Minx looking for somewhere to stay, slept in the car at nights. Everywhere we went there were signs. *No blacks, no children*. One landlady was more poetic. *No blacks, no picaninnies*. To this day when I feel miserable and abandoned I curl up for the night in the back of my car. Are you in favour of discrimination? Against blacks, against children?

ENOCH. Every molecule in my body is prejudiced. Said Powell, beginning to enjoy himself.

ROSE. You admit it.

ENOCH. Every molecule in every body is prejudiced in favour of its own survival. There is nothing irrational about prejudice.

ROSE. How do I threaten your survival?

ENOCH. You pursue your own.

ROSE. You said it's a conflict of meaning.

ENOCH. You rob me of England. What it means to me.

ROSE. So you want to expel me.

ENOCH. It's not within my power.

ROSE. Infuriating, isn't it. That's what pushes the racist to extremes. His powerlessness. He pushes excrement through the letter box of his enemy but when he goes home there's the very faint smell of shit clinging to his fingers. Isn't there? There's no getting rid of it. His disgust. Or if not literally excrement through letter boxes he makes speeches which serve the same purpose. The only way he can sustain his identity is through conflict, so he goes on and on. Addicted.

ENOCH. And you. Do you wish to expel *me*?

ROSE. I wouldn't use that word.

ENOCH. You wish no part of me.

The tape recorder.

ROSE. No, I'm afraid I don't.

ENOCH. How fragile is the political community.

ROSE. Yes.

ENOCH. Especially when as now there are forces working against integration.

ROSE. You're one of them.

ENOCH. Did I create Muslim terrorists? This genocidal war in Bosnia. There are *mujahideen* fighting for the Bosnian Muslims who speak in broad Manchester and London accents.

ROSE. You disinherited them.

ENOCH. Muslims recruited at universities in London. King's College, Tower Hamlets College, School of Oriental and African Studies, young educated Muslims who take humanitarian aid to Bosnia and stay to fight a *jihad*.

ROSE. They have seen young educated European Muslims like themselves being ethnically cleansed.

ENOCH. What do you suppose will happen when they come home?

ROSE. I don't think they'll start a *jihad*.

ENOCH. Will they be different from you and me?

ROSE. In a way.

ENOCH. Will they have different beliefs?

ROSE. It's not about believing it's about belonging.

ENOCH. To what will they belong?

ROSE. You call people aliens for twenty years, don't be surprised if you alienate them.

ENOCH. They will belong to the *ummah*, they will fight as they are fighting now for the Caliphate. They may live in England but they will not dwell here.

ROSE. The tiniest fraction of the Muslim population.

ENOCH. That is all it takes to create terror and divide communities. Look at the IRA.

ROSE. In the last war more than a hundred thousand Muslims fought. Punjabi regiments fought beside the Berkshires, died beside the Devonshires. Could we create a shared identity out of that?

ENOCH. I fear no one understands not the scale of the crisis we face but its nature. Its character. The lack of attachment. You would agree would you not that the essence of nationhood is a feeling among its subdivisions that they are parts of a greater whole. A huge proportion of the people are a stranger to that feeling. Young people, intellectuals, liberals, the left.

ROSE. We are constantly under attack.

ENOCH. Ah. You are a persecuted minority?

ROSE. The facts speak for themselves. Young black people three times more likely to be unemployed than white.

ENOCH. And would the immigrant-descended population
would unemployed young Muslims open their arms to a
fresh wave of immigrants?

ROSE. You're ignoring the substantive point about differentials.

ENOCH. It almost passes belief such figures are gathered.

ROSE. They confirm a suspicion of unfairness.

ENOCH. Let me understand your meaning. You propose not to
reduce the total number of unemployed but to redistribute
unemployment more fairly.

ROSE. You're making mischief.

ENOCH. You mustn't try to read me, I am volcanic with anger.
Poor white males in Oldham are as unemployed as poor
Muslim males. To make division between the unemployed of
one colour and the unemployed of another is racist. It is the
communalism about which I warned in the Birmingham
speech. Each community claiming special rights, endlessly
keeping score of injustices done

They start talking over each other.

ROSE. *claiming* equal rights?

ENOCH. keeping score and point-scoring (I did not say equal
rights)

ROSE. *yes* we claim equal rights

ENOCH. *special* rights, I said *special* rights

ROSE. if no one keeps a record of injustices done

ENOCH. point-scoring and a descent into meaningless babble

ROSE. no point in talking, you are beyond the pale.

This stops them.

ENOCH. I was a Member of Parliament elected by my fellow
countrymen for four decades; on the question of identity
I speak for perhaps half the English working class. If I am
beyond the pale, so are they, and so, it follows, is democracy.

The conversation has gone nowhere.

ROSE. Will we leave it here?

ENOCH. Shall we?

ROSE. Don't see where we're going.

ENOCH. No.

ROSE. Pointless.

ENOCH. Where next for you?

ROSE. Giving a paper to a conference in Aberystwyth.

ENOCH. About what?

ROSE. Hatred.

ENOCH. Ah. This is a field trip. I hope you visit Warwick first, it's the town in England I've always been happiest. Take your friend to see the castle.

ROSE *has nothing on tape to give* SOFIA. *She's failed her.*

ROSE. Talk to me.

ENOCH. You prefer my company to your friend's.

ROSE. I feel like I've killed something. Why did you ask to meet me here?

ENOCH. This is where I'll be buried. In my brigadier uniform.

ROSE. Are these war graves?

ENOCH. Yes.

ROSE. Are any of them black?

She looks at the first tomb.

Raymond Antoine Penna, Pioneer Corps.

She looks at the second tomb.

Stanislaw Rzegocki, Polish Resettlement Corps.

She goes to the third tomb.

John Francis Sheedy, Royal Engineers.

The fourth tomb.

W.S. Lawrence. First Class Boy HMS Barham. 1924-1941.

He wished to die for England.

His parents. His thoughts. Seventeen!

She is moved.

ENOCH. I should like to have died in the war. But at least I shall be buried beside my comrades. We long for identity. It's like the longing for a soul.

ROSE. My parents met in Cricklewood working for the railway. There were two sheds then; Mum was a typist in the steam shed, Dad an electrician in the diesel, lunch breaks he used to cross the tracks to chat her up. Went to look for the sheds last week. Everything solid melts into air.

ENOCH. The need to hold on to something.

ROSE. To belong.

ENOCH. Do you belong?

ROSE. No. Do you?

ENOCH. What became of your parents?

ROSE. My mother went to Wolverhampton so my father couldn't find me.

ROSE *goes to gather up her tape recorder, knowing she has nothing of any use. She tries one last thing.*

Listen; we'll never agree in a million years, you and me…

ENOCH. You and I. No.

ROSE.…imagine we were advising other people, how to heal a divide. What would we suggest?

ENOCH. Do these putative people *wish* to overcome their differences?

ROSE. No.

ENOCH. We might tell them everything in life is done through persuasion. To be isolated is by definition a sign of failure, in public or in private life.

ROSE *hears the admission of failure implicit in his words.*

ROSE. Yes.

ENOCH. What keeps these two persons apart?

ROSE. Let's imagine their hatred is overwhelming. Like a husband and wife.

ENOCH. What is the substance of their argument?

ROSE. Something terrible intractable...

ENOCH. The custody of a child perhaps? In order to win custody hearings, parents vilify each other, cast up the past. And when the court makes its decision, neither is happy. No matter how much of the child they're given it's not enough.

ROSE. The child's their identity.

A slight change in the tenor of their discussion now that it's struck upon the essential question. There's a tension; the closer they come to an understanding the more tense they feel and the more tentative the steps they take.

ENOCH. Their identity. Yes.

ROSE. How would things improve?

ENOCH. The more of the child you want the more, as the father, I shall be enraged.

ROSE. Yes but if you were an adviser to the father.

ENOCH. I should say that in the end the child comes first. Go to the mother, offer to put your differences aside.

What would you do if the father came to you, the mother?

ROSE. I would be sick afraid.

ENOCH. Of what?

ROSE. What I might lose. When you start having a conversation. When you listen. You change.

So, you agree I'm English.

ENOCH. I wasn't aware I'd made any such admission.

ROSE. You agreed the child was ours.

ENOCH. Let us accept you and I have a child. The question arises *Which of us best knows the child?* I might say to the Court *But Your Honour, she drinks. Her memory of events is not to be trusted. The account she gives the Court must be treated with circumspection, even suspicion.*

ROSE. Is your recollection of events perfect?

ENOCH. If I cannot depend on my own memories, on what ground do I stand? Since the age of five I have made it my study to know myself.

ROSE. Knowledge, even self-knowledge. There are large blanks. I had an experience recently. Take this moment now. How can I see me? You can see me better than I can. Some ways possibly, see me better than I can.

That's not easy to say.

And you, at this moment you're half-blind.

ENOCH. I can see perfectly.

ROSE. What does your face look like?

What's behind you?

For ENOCH *to turn would take a long time.*

I see what you can't, you see what I can't. That's the thing about knowledge. Where is it?

ENOCH. Where is it?

ROSE. Yes.

ENOCH. In economics we say *knowledge is dispersed.* Everyone holds a piece of the jigsaw. How might this help our reflections on identity.

ROSE. We could ask who defines Englishness. At the beginning of this conversation *you* did.

ENOCH. Who to your mind *should* define Englishness?

ROSE. The English.

ENOCH. And who are the English?

ROSE. The English are the people who live here.

ENOCH. There was a poll in the *Observer* last week. A majority of British Muslims say they are Muslim first British second.

ROSE. I imagine the majority of British mothers would say they were mothers first British second. We all have multiple identities, English is what we share.

ENOCH. Would you accept some of us are more English than others?

ROSE. In our souls?

ENOCH. In our understanding. What in your view is the quintessence of Englishness?

ROSE. The quintessence of Englishness is this.

She gives him the Vicky, or a 'get it right up you' arm. Silence. He grows to full height.

ENOCH. I am dismayed. We are of one mind on this matter. What then is England?

ROSE. Nothing is fixed. England is the relationship between us.

ENOCH. Between you and me?

ROSE. Between us all.

ENOCH. Why is that difficult to say?

ROSE. When your community meets my community, you know one half of the story, we know the other. We keep each other honest.

ENOCH. A little like primates grooming each other.

ROSE. Yes.

ENOCH. Turn off the tape. I have something to say on the subject of the Birmingham speech.

ROSE *turns off the tape*.

ROSE. It's off.

He begins to tremor. We hardly see it at first.

ENOCH. I wish to say this. No one else can know what it was like to have made that speech; just as no one can know what it is like to be Salman Rushdie except Salman Rushdie.

His tremor intensifies.

Thucydides uses a phrase υπο φυσεως αναγχαιας, which describes what is beyond individual human power to cause or control. I was a storm. I was also a man entirely alone in a storm. I was a force that tore up trees and blew down chimneys, at the selfsame moment I was a man walking the streets as the chimneys fell and smashed on the road. There were forces beyond my control and I was one of them.

He's shaking uncontrollably.

I was a hurricane. We christen hurricanes for the sake of reference and to give ourselves the illusion we understand them. Hurricane Enoch, Hurricane Rushdie. There will be more hurricanes to come and they will be given different names, but I warn you; when they occur no one will hear a word that's spoken.

The tremor subsides. SOFIA *enters*.

ROSE *offers her the tape recorder.*

ROSE. Looking forward to Aberystwyth now. I love the seaside out of season, puts you in the mood for dying. Here.

SOFIA. You got something.

ROSE. Yes.

SOFIA. You got something.

ROSE. Yes.

SOFIA *takes the tape recorder.*

SOFIA. You got something.

ROSE. Yes.

Call of a lapwing.

ENOCH. Listen. The call of a lapwing.

SOFIA. Yes. In winter they flock near my croft. They love the easy-going land. The untouchable peace. They sound different up there. On a desolate shore their cries go right through you.

ENOCH. On your way to Aberystwyth you must stop in Shropshire and look for the lapwing. The hills above the River Onny, young as the lambs. Like the Ice Age is over and England is born.

Ends.

A Nick Hern Book

What Shadows first published in Great Britain in 2016 as a paperback original by Nick Hern Books Limited, The Glasshouse, 49a Goldhawk Road, London W12 8QP, in association with Birmingham Repertory Theatre

Reprinted with a new cover in 2017

Cover image: Getty Images/Jonathan Stamp

Designed and typeset by Nick Hern Books, London
Printed in the UK by Mimeo Ltd, Huntingdon, Cambridgeshire PE29 6XX

A CIP catalogue record for this book is available from the British Library

ISBN   978 1 84842 627 6